DOORWAYS TO A
DEEPER FAITH

A Gift for You
From:
Bishop Marian D. Hickman,
Bishop Brandon Thompson, and
Pastor Sandra Forney
2007 God Bless You!

Other books by Alan Kent Scholes
The Artful Dodger: A Skeptic Confronts Christianity
*What Christianity is All About: How You Can Know and
Enjoy God*

DOORWAYS TO A
DEEPER FAITH

Six Keys to a Closer Walk with God

ALAN KENT SCHOLES

Baker Books

A Division of Baker Book House Co
Grand Rapids, Michigan 49516

© 2002 by Alan Kent Scholes

Published by Baker Books
a division of Baker Book House Company
P.O. Box 6287, Grand Rapids, MI 49516-6287

Printed in the United States of America

Library of Congress Cataloging-in-Publication Data

Scholes, Alan Kent, 1947–
    Doorways to a deeper faith : six keys to a closer walk with God / Alan
Kent Scholes.
        p.   cm.
    Includes bibliographical references
    ISBN: 0-8010-6392-2 (pbk.)
    1. Christian life. I. Title: Deeper faith. II. Title.

BV4501.3 .S36 2002
248.4—dc21   2001058958

For current information about all releases from Baker Book House, visit our web site:
                      http://www.bakerbooks.com

To the Darling of my heart, my loving wife,
Janice Lynn Penrose Scholes
You believed in this from the beginning
and saw it through to the finish

CONTENTS

ACKNOWLEDGMENTS

The seed of the idea that grew into this book was planted in my heart and mind more than thirty years ago by Dr. Bill Bright. It has always impressed me how warmly he introduces leaders from other ministries, even when they speak about the Christian life very differently than we normally do in Campus Crusade. Thank you, Bill, for consistently modeling a gracious appreciation for others in Christ's body.

Tom Carter, now home with the Lord, suggested some of the ideas in this book during long discussions my third year on staff. I'm grateful to Tom for stimulating my thoughts and patiently listening and discussing them with me during their gestation.

Though I've shared these concepts with many groups for the past thirty years, I doubt that I would have put them in book form if not for the encouragement of two old friends. Several years ago when I visited Curt Fenz in Budapest, Hungary, we started reminiscing about his first year on Campus Crusade staff. Curt said, "One of the things I remember from that year was when you shared with the team about doors into faith." Thanks, Curt, for doing me the honor of remembering something I said so many years ago and graciously encouraging me with the memory.

It was only a couple of months after my visit with Curt that my longtime friend Rich Poll said, "Alan, I'm gonna keep buggin' you 'til you put that doors into faith idea into a book!" Thanks, Rich, for the right word at the right time. You have my permission to bug me anytime on any subject!

Even with my two friends' encouragement, I doubt the book would have been written without the wise counsel of my friend, agent, and fellow Plot 'n Blot Society member, Janet Grant. I'm grateful, Janet, that you saw the potential and helped me mold the idea into a coherent book.

My theology class in the spring of 2001 dissected the manuscript and made many helpful suggestions from a wide range of cultural and ministry perspectives. Thanks to Jonathan Coody, Chiyoko Furukawa, Mate Gyori, MeeKyung Kim, Daniel Kopp, Fredrick Outa, John Reutener, Kurt Ritz, Jason Taylor, Andrew Yarbrough, and Jie Zong. Thanks also to my colleague Lewis Winkler who helped teach the class and offered a number of valuable insights. Special thanks to Jane Miller and Alice Penrose for spending much of their vacation proofreading the entire manuscript.

But the greatest contributors to this book have been the members of the Doors into Faith study group who met each week and faithfully read and critiqued each page and each chapter as it grew. Thanks to Becky Beavers, Tom and Teri Newcombe, Darrel and Sue Parks, and Jerry Pitts. And special endurance medals to those who hung in for the entire eighteen months and two hundred pages. I'm deeply grateful to Mike Beavers, Liann McCreery, Teresa Radsick, Alan and Gail Russell, and Kathie Slusser. You were encouraging, patient, vulnerable, and insightful. You praised me when I got it right and told me when I missed the mark. Who could ask for truer friends?

My insightful wife, Jan, was the one who first conceived the idea for a group to workshop the book. Thank you for knowing me so well and helping provide what it would take to bring this to completion. Truly, this book is yours as much as mine.

ONE

JUST A CLOSER WALK WITH THEE

I hope you can help me," Brittany[1] said. "My life feels hopeless."

We were sitting on a concrete bench outside my college dorm late on a fall afternoon. Though her face was heavily made-up, it was round and beautiful. A single tear rimmed a pale blue eye. "I quit going to church when I was twelve—my dad was gone by then and my mom didn't attend much after he left. I started dating high school boys when I was thirteen. At first, it was just a couple of beers and heavy petting in the backseat, but pretty soon it was hard drugs—then one of my boyfriends began to hit me."

She lowered her head and seemed unable to speak for a moment. "I should have left him. . . . But I guess it was better than no attention at all."

She went on for twenty minutes. A pregnancy at fifteen, then an abortion. A night in jail after a drug-party raid. Verbal battles with her mom followed by days of angry silence.

Brittany had found Christ as a junior in high school and her grades had improved enough for her to get into the state college we were both attending. I was the student leader of the small Campus Crusade for Christ group, and one of her friends had suggested she talk to me.

"Alan, I'm afraid I'm going to flunk out! I just can't seem to concentrate. Sometimes when I'm studying, I get these flashbacks, even though I've been clean for almost three years.

"And the worst part is God seems so distant—not like when I was a new believer. I try to pray but I have no idea if he even hears me anymore. Many nights I end up depressed, crying into some textbook." Her eyes looked like slate as she stared at me. "Can you help me?"

As a young believer myself, I was not sure how to answer. Finally I mumbled, "You just need to have faith."

I could sense her disappointment and frustration. She needed more from me, but on that day I had no more to give her.

The conversation with Brittany has haunted me ever since. Not surprisingly, I never saw her again. In years since, I thought many times about what I should have said. Clearly the first thing I should have done was admitted that I had no idea how to help her! But what sort of answer might I give her today, after thirty years in ministry? To begin with, I now believe she was struggling with not just one problem but several. Today I would tell her that I strongly suspect some of her problems might require more than I as a theologian and spiritual counselor could give her.[2]

But what spiritual advice would I give her today, instead of "just have faith"? First, I've realized that, in one sense, my answer to Brittany was not entirely wrong. *Faith* is the central word the Bible uses to describe how we come into and continue an intimate, personal, growing relationship with God. I was not wrong to tell her that faith was the key to a closer relationship with God. But I've also realized that for most Christians, the advice "just have faith" is too vague and amorphous to be helpful. It's like trying to capture a morning mist and take it home with you in a jar.

Since that college conversation, I've met many Christians who see a life of faith as a far-off, impossible goal, something only super-Christians or ministers can do. But I've also met many quite ordinary believers who are consistently walking with Christ and growing in their life of faith. Often the difference is that the growing believers have been taught or have discovered one or more of the biblical secrets for growth, which I call "doors into faith."

God knew that most of us would not immediately grasp what he meant by faith. He knew that most of us are like Brittany; we need something more concrete, more tangible, more practical, something we can visualize, grab onto, and use. So he placed in the Scripture a number of tangible descriptions of what faith feels, tastes, and acts like. These are vivid pictures of what it means to walk closely with him. I think he also knew that no one door would be equally helpful to people with varied backgrounds, temperaments, family experiences, and relationships. So he sprinkled a number of very different kinds of doors throughout the Bible.

In this book we will look in some detail at six of these doors:

- Be Who You Really Are (Position in Christ). The apostle Paul tells us that we have died and been raised with Christ. We have a new nature and can now resist the temptations of our old nature and live like the new people we really are.

- Let Your Pride Be Broken (Death to Self). Though God is not the author of pain and suffering, he often uses difficult circumstances and even hurts from others to break down our pride and trust in ourselves so that his life can flow freely through us.
- Open Yourself to Love (Under Grace). We can live lives that truly please God only when we live in a loving reponse to God's free gift. We cannot please God by our performance; he is already pleased with us because of Christ.
- Let Christ Live through You (Exchanged Life). The Christian life is not difficult—it's impossible! Only one Person ever lived it on this earth. And only one Person is able to live it today. The Bible teaches that the secret of Christianity is that Christ lives in and through the believer.
- Become a True Disciple (Disciplined Life). Serious growth in the Christian life must eventually involve discipline. Discipline is not God's punishment when we do wrong; rather it is God's loving plan for us to grow ever closer to him.
- Walk in the Spirit (Spirit Filled). The fullness and power of God's Holy Spirit—of God Himself—can be ours simply by believing what the Bible teaches about being filled. We can be filled with the Spirit by confessing all known sins and appropriating the fullness by faith.

I believe the Bible actually contains more than six doors to faith, but I've chosen to concentrate on these because they all have been at the center of the teaching of prominent speakers, popular writers, and, in some cases, influential movements during the last two centuries. If you have learned your walk of faith through one of the biblical doors, it is very likely to be one of these six.

For Believers Only

One of my graduate students raised his hand. "So let me see if I have this straight. These doors into faith are different ways people come to Christ. Is that right?" He must have seen a look of disappointment on my face, because quickly he added, "Or not."

The class had been reading and discussing the rough draft of this book.

"How many of the rest of you understood the book that way?" I asked.

A couple of other hands went up.

"Well," I said, "I can see I still have some work to do."

There's an old saying in education that the teacher always learns more from the students than the students do from the teacher. It was certainly true that day.

What I learned is that if I'm not careful, my idea of doors into faith can be pretty confusing.

So let me say it as directly as I can. This is not a book for nonbelievers. This book won't give you tips on how to witness to your neighbor. This book would not make a good gift for your unsaved Aunt Hilda. This book does not describe different ways people find Christ. I can recommend several such books, but this is not one of them.[3] So if you're looking for a book about salvation, put this one down and keep looking.

However, if you are already a Christian, then this book may be just what you want. You may be a new believer, just starting out in your walk of faith. Or maybe you have been a Christian a while but would like a more consistent and fulfilling walk with the Lord. You may have begun your walk of faith a number of years ago (perhaps through one of these six doors) but now feel your Christian life is "just not working" like it used to. You may wonder why some Christians talk about their Christian life in language that is very different from yours. Or you may want to help others grow in their walk with the Lord.

If any of these sound like you, read on.

Transition Time

Before we explore the six doors, I want to make some general observations about the Christian life as a whole. I became a Christian more than thirty years ago in 1966. That was before a human first set foot on the moon, before Watergate, before the assassination of Martin Luther King Jr., and before terrorists destroyed the Twin Towers. But thirty years is really a very short period of time. The Bible tells us that we Christians are going to live eternally, forever! The last stanza of "Amazing Grace" puts it well.

> When we've been there ten thousand years . . .
> We've no less days . . . than when we first begun.

John Newton *could* have used ten million or ten billion. After you and I have lived ten *trillion years,* we will still be able to truthfully say, "We've just begun."

Even if you manage to live 152 years before your body dies, and even if you became a Christian as a child of two, your 150 years as a Christian on this planet will be only a tiny portion of your entire life. Seen in that light, the years between the time you receive Christ and the time you go home to be with him are only a tiny parenthesis, a wink of an eye.

In fact the Bible portrays the years of our Christian life on this earth as a kind of transition period. It is a transition between our former life without Christ and the eons of eternity we will spend fully united with him. But what kind of transition is it?

As I write these words, I am rejoicing that this past weekend my son, Rich, became engaged to a wonderful young woman named Molly.[4] The date for the wedding has been set for next summer, nine months away. He and I were talking on the phone this morning about plans for the wedding, plans for the honeymoon, and their plans for their life together. This next nine months will be exciting, challenging, and, undoubtedly, sometimes difficult. It is a time of transition. Rich and Molly are not yet married but neither are they exactly single anymore. People will begin to treat them differently than they did when they were "eligible." Now they are "spoken for"; they belong to each other.

The Bible uses the image of engagement or betrothal to describe the lives of believers in the church. We will be the bride of Christ (John 3:29; Rev. 19:7) and are currently waiting for the wedding feast, which will happen when Christ returns to take us home (Rev. 19:9).

To understand any of the doors into faith we must grasp the temporary and transitional nature of our current lives. We need to understand how our lives in this "engagement" period are different from what we experienced before we knew Christ. It is also crucial that we know how our lives will change when the "marriage" comes and we are his forever. The Bible says that now we see God as if through a dark and dim mirror (1 Cor. 13:12a). But when Christ returns for his bride, then we will see him "face to face" (v. 12b). Paul says that then we will know him as intimately as he now knows us (v. 12c)! Then the short transitional period of living by faith will be over and an eternity of unhindered relationship will have begun.

Door Problems

Unfortunately, in this transition time we are all still fallen creatures living in a fallen world. And that means we have to live with some irksome difficulties connected with the existence of the doors into faith. Some believers have entered through a particular door and feel that all believers must come to a life of faith exactly as they did. Others cannot understand why everyone doesn't find their favorite door as effective as they do. It is sad that some believers have been taught a particular door but have misunderstood it and, though sincerely trying to enter, have missed the life of faith. As I present the six doors in the upcoming chapters, my hope is that among them you will find the door that is most helpful for you to enter a consistent life of faith.

Along the way you're going to meet Sarah, who wishes she could take her own life; Rex, who wants out of law school; Gabrielle, who's trying to survive her comforters; and Jonathan, who finds the Christian life way too hard. You'll ride the jet stream to Hong Kong, get stranded in Moscow, and sip cappuccino with a genuine postmodern Christian in California.

So hold on. I think you'll find there's nothing as disturbing, exciting, frustrating, and exhilarating as a true-life adventure of faith.

TWO

HOW MUCH FAITH IS ENOUGH?

Chelsea wrinkled her nose and shrugged her shoulders. "I've tried living the Christian life. But it doesn't seem to work for me anymore—I guess I just don't have enough faith!" Chelsea was raised in a Christian home and had been active in her church youth group and in a Christian club at her high school. But now she was midway through her first year in a secular college, two hundred miles from her parents.

"At home it seemed pretty easy to be a Christian." She looked away, as if uncomfortable with my gaze. "But here there are so many new and exciting temptations . . . it really takes a lot of faith to live like a Christian on this campus. I'm afraid I've done it all. Booze, drugs, sex. You name it. My parents will be so disgusted if they ever find out. And they won't understand. They have tons of faith. Me, it seems like I have hardly any."

"May I ask you a question?" I said.

"Sure, I guess."

"You said you don't have much faith. If you wanted more, how do you think you could go about getting it?"

Chelsea brushed brown bangs away from her eyes. "I . . . I'm not sure. I guess I could pray for more faith. Isn't there a verse somewhere that says faith is a gift from God? Maybe we just have to wait until God gives us more faith."

"You're right about the verse," I said. "Ephesians 2:8 says that faith is a gift from God. But I don't think the answer is to pray for more faith."

"You don't?" She looked puzzled.

I smiled. "Would it surprise you if I told you that you already have all the faith you need to deal with the temptations you face here on campus?"

"I do?"

"Chelsea, if you've genuinely received Christ, in that moment, God gave you all the faith you'll ever need."

"Hmm . . . it sure doesn't feel that way to me."

Like Chelsea, many Christians believe that their problem is that they "just don't have enough faith." They look at faith as a commodity, like money, which some believers have more of than others.

But the Bible pictures faith as an attitude, an attitude of trust. As we explore the doors into faith in this book, we will discover a recurring theme. Opening up our faith is not a process of convincing God to give us more of what we need to live the Christian life. Rather, living the Christian life is a process of learning how to use more of what God has already given us!

Risky Business

There is a second theme we will see repeated as we venture through the various doors of faith. We will discover that a life of faith often includes risk.

Recently Jacob, a successful businessman, asked me an intriguing question. "Does faith always have to involve risk?"

"That's a rather profound question," I said. "I don't think anyone's ever asked me that before. Hmm . . . before I try to answer, may I ask you a question?"

Jacob angled his head and regarded me with one eye. "Stalling?"

"Maybe," I grinned. "But I'm curious. Why do you want to know?"

Jacob frowned. "Because I've never found risk easy. In my business I always make sure I'm well prepared for any situation. I never meet with a client unless I'm completely ready. And I never make a commitment unless I'm sure I can follow through and deliver."

"So, if I understand you," I said, "it sounds like you avoid risk in your business whenever you can."

"Exactly. As far as I'm concerned, risk is a bad thing that I try to avoid as often as possible!" He smiled. "So what about it, Doc? Is there always risk in faith?"

"Well, now that you've given me a minute to consider your question, I think I would have to answer no. I don't think risk is a necessary ingredient of faith."

"Why not?"

"The primary reason is something Paul says about faith in 1 Corinthians."

"Which is?"

"At the end of chapter 13, where Paul has been telling the Corinthians that all the spiritual gifts will eventually be done away with and cease, he goes on to mention some things that will continue forever. Do you remember what those are?"

Jacob got a faraway look in his eye. "I know he says that *love* will go on forever. Is that what you mean?"

"Exactly right! He also lists two other things that will remain or endure—hope and *faith*."

He still looked puzzled. "Okay. But I don't see how that answers my question."

"Well, in just the previous verse, Paul said, 'Now we see but a poor reflection as in a mirror; then we shall see face to face. Now I know in part; then I shall know fully, even as I am fully known" (1 Cor. 13:12 NIV).

Jacob shrugged. "So, I guess that means, when Christ returns, we won't need spiritual gifts anymore, but we'll still have faith."

"That's right. And that makes sense if we understand that *faith* in the Bible just means trust. When we are home with him, we'll still trust God; in fact our faith, or our trust, will be perfected. But much, or perhaps all, of the risk that our faith involves in this life will be gone."

"I get it," he said. "So our faith, or trust, in heaven won't involve much risk. But what about here and now?"

"Well," I said, "that's a different matter. I think most Christian faith in our present world does require a greater or lesser degree of risk."

"That's what I was afraid of," said Jacob, with a sigh.

Wedding Rehearsal

Why does faith in our current world feel so risky? In the last chapter I said that our Christian life here on earth is a time of transition, which is why the Bible compares it to the period of betrothal or engagement. We are no longer exactly of the world, but we are also not as fully Christ's as we someday will be. I think that grasping the temporary, transitional nature of our Christian life on this earth can go a long way toward helping us understand why faith can seem scary, why faith often involves risk.

The great "Hall of Faith" in the Bible, Hebrews, chapter 11, begins with a definition of faith. "Now faith is being sure of what we hope for and certain of what we do not see" (Heb. 11:1 NIV). It's clear that the writer is not talking about faith in the world to come where we *will* see so much that is now hidden. He's talking about our walk of faith as believers in our present world. And that's exactly where a lot of the risk enters in. If we could clearly see the future consequences of our sin, and also the wonderful rewards of obedience, resisting temptation would not seem risky at all. If we had the magnificent resurrected Christ standing in front of us in all his love, majesty, and power, it would not seem nearly so difficult or scary to trust him with our temporary struggles.

But that is not our current situation. In our present world, "we walk by faith, not by sight" (2 Cor. 5:7). To begin with, we have to trust a Person we cannot see. We also have to live with a view of the world that is contrary to much of what the society around us thinks—perhaps even contrary to the views of our closest friends and family. Often what Christ asks us to do goes against all our instincts and even our own best human judgment. The good news is that this troublesome situation is only temporary. When we are with Christ, we *will* see the One we are trusting. Christ himself will remake the world order so that it will support truth, love, and justice. Then it will be easy to see that his teachings have really been the most sensible all along. But in the meantime, in this transition period called the Christian life, what he says and asks often seem unreasonable.

Before every wedding I've ever been a part of, there has been a wedding rehearsal. There are, of course, very practical reasons for this. One is simply so everyone will know where to stand, when to speak, and so forth. But there is another benefit to the wedding rehearsal. I think it tends to reduce the anxiety the bride and/or groom may tend to be feeling right before the wedding. In a larger sense, the whole engagement period is (or should be) a kind of rehearsal for marriage. During that time a couple is getting better acquainted with each other and with each other's friends and family. If the couple is wise, they will spend time learning about each other's likes and dislikes, plans, hopes, and, perhaps, fears concerning the future. They have the opportunity to grow in emotional and personal maturity so they will be ready for the responsibilities and challenges of marriage.

Our Christian life here on earth is exactly that sort of transitional period. We have a chance to grow to know Christ better. We have a chance to discover the unique gifts and abilities God has given us. We can learn to work harmoniously within the church, Christ's eternal family. We can grow toward the sort of spiritual maturity that will prepare us to be citizens of God's kingdom.

Pride or Fear

"Can I . . . ?" Kaitlyn looked around, as if worried someone else would hear. "Can I ask you a question?"

I had just finished teaching the adult Sunday school class. Everyone else had left for church and I was sorting my notes and stashing them away in my carrying case. Apparently Kaitlyn had waited in the back of the room until everyone else had gone. Though she'd attended my class for months, she always sat in the back row and never entered into any of the class discussions.

"Sure," I said and pulled over two chairs.

"Well," Kaitlyn said, once we were seated, "my . . . my question is about the sermon last week." She did not raise her eyes to meet mine and she kept twisting her hands in her lap. This was obviously hard for her.

"The sermon," I said, trying to sound encouraging. "Yes, I was here last week."

"Well, it was a very good sermon. Very good. It's just . . . well, there was something I didn't exactly understand. I'm sure everyone else did. And I didn't want to bother the pastor about it. So I was hoping . . . since you're my Sunday school teacher, I was hoping you . . ."

Kaitlyn's gaze flicked up toward my face and then retreated back down into her lap.

"Of course," I said. "I'll be glad to help if I can."

There was a long, uncomfortable silence. I couldn't think of anything appropriate to say.

"Well, there was that part where he talked about pride."

"Yes, I remember."

"Pastor said pride was the root sin and all other sins come from it."

"That's right," I agreed. "That's what he said."

"And he said that even when someone was shy and quiet that it was just a cover-up for the pride that was lurking under the surface."

"Yes, he did make a comment like that."

"Well, that's the problem I don't understand. I mean, I know I'm a sinner, a terrible sinner. But I've never thought my problem was pride."

Kaitlyn was quiet for a moment, considering.

"Or is it proud of me to say that? I don't believe for a minute that I'm better than anyone else. I know I'm not. I've got plenty of problems. I just never realized pride was one of them."

"Kaitlyn," I said, "I don't know you very well. But I think it's safe to say you don't need to spend any time or energy worrying about a serious pride problem."

It has been pretty common in evangelical circles, for at least the last fifty years, to say that pride is the root sin. And the biblical case is not hard to make. It appears that Satan's original fall involved pride (Isa. 14:12–14). It also looks like the serpent's temptation of Eve in the Garden was at least partially a temptation to pride (Gen. 3:6).

So for a Bible teacher or preacher to say that pride is the first sin (either in the universe or in the human race) is not much of a stretch. But now here's where it gets a little tricky. Many evangelical teachers have not been content simply to say that pride was the first sin. They go on to assert that it is the root of all sin and therefore every sin is based on pride or somehow derives from pride. I do not believe that the Bible anywhere clearly teaches that idea. Nowhere does the Bible say that pride is the root of all evil. In the King James translation, 1 Timothy 6:10 says that "the love of money is the root of all evil." Teachers who want to defend the pride-as-the-root-sin theory are quick to point out that love of money is just another form of pride. There are two problems with this assertion. First, Paul does not say that the love of money and pride are the same thing, much less that the love of money comes from pride. Paul does mention pride in verse 4, but there he is talking about teachers of false doctrine, not about money.

But there is an even bigger problem in trying to use 1 Timothy to prove that pride is the root sin or even that there is any sin that is at the root of all the others. The problem is that the King James Version is not an entirely accurate translation of the New Testament Greek Paul actually wrote. A more faithful translation would be "the love of money is a root of all sorts of evil." This is the way the New American Standard version translates the verse.[1] That's far less sweeping, isn't it? The love of money is *a* root, not *the* root. And what is it a root of? "All sorts of evil." Not "all evil." Suppose you asked me what I studied in college and I answered, "Oh, all sorts of subjects." Would you presume from my answer that in my four years of college I had studied every subject known to humanity? Of course not. You'd know that I meant many subjects or a wide variety or a diverse selection, something like that. And this is exactly what Paul is trying to say about the love of money leading to evil. He's not trying to say that the love of money is the one and only source of every evil in existence. Rather he's saying that the love of money leads to many different kinds of evils.

By now you may be asking, "Alan, what's your point?" It's just this. I don't think pride is the root sin or the sin that is somehow lurking behind every other.

Kaitlyn was exactly right. She had problems but they weren't all related to pride. In fact, from her manner, I'd guess pride was not her problem at all. From the way she behaved in class and her body language the day she talked to me, I'd guess Kaitlyn's root problem was fear.

It has always fascinated me that after the fall, the first sign that anything was wrong with Adam and Eve was not that they reacted with pride. Instead, they responded with fear. God comes looking for Adam and asks, "Where are you?" What is Adam's response? He says, "I was afraid because I was naked; so I hid myself" (Gen. 3:10).

Why is it, then, that so many in the evangelical world have taught that pride is the root sin? Let me give you an educated guess. I'm guessing that one reason is that the vast majority of evangelical writers and preachers have been men.

Let me explain what I mean. I have observed that in Europe and North America it is much more common for men to struggle with pride as their primary form of unbelief than for women to struggle with it. It is also more common for women to fall short of faith through fear. Of course there are many exceptions on both sides. There are some men who are quite timid and fearful and some women who are assertive and prideful. And I'm not at all sure how much of this is an innate difference and how much is cultural and learned.

One of the things that makes me hesitate to conclude that the difference is innate is the Genesis account we just looked at. The first fallen human to exhibit a fear response was not a woman but Adam. It is also possible that male Christian leaders have an even greater tendency to struggle with pride (as opposed to fear) than the general male Christian population.

In any case, my theory is that if women had been writing all those books and giving all those sermons for the last fifty or a hundred years, we'd have heard a lot less about pride and a lot more about fear.

All of this is going to be important as we begin to explore the various doors into faith. I'm convinced that at least as many people have failed to find the true attitude of faith through fear as have through pride. Perhaps in Western culture, more women have fallen short of faith through fear and more men through pride. Whether that is true or not, both are dangers to watch out for as we seek to find doors into a genuine walk of faith.

How about You?

Where are you in your Christian life and walk? Are you a new believer just now starting to take your first steps of faith? Or maybe you have known Christ for many years but have often been tripped up by pride or fear. Maybe you too sometimes feel a little like Chelsea or Jacob. Perhaps you struggle to really grasp what it means to live by faith. Or maybe you know other believers—family, friends, people in your church—who are frustrated in their Christian walk. I wrote this book primarily for Chelsea, Jacob, Kaitlyn, and all the other Christians like them who have struggled with living the Christian life.

In the next few chapters, I'm going to introduce six doors or pictures of faith. Any of these doors can lead to a closer walk with God, but each of us is attracted to different doors because of our personality, upbringing, or previous Christian experience. Which door will open wide to a deeper understanding of God? Only you can say. But if you are discouraged or struggling in your Christian life—

or if you just want a deeper faith—my prayer is that you will find one or more of the doors that will help you enter into a consistent walk with the Lord.

This chapter is a brief introduction to the nature of faith. Later in the book, I will develop more fully some of the ideas introduced here. I will attempt a more complete definition of faith. I'll explore more fully the relationship between faith, risk, and reason. And I'll give some practical tips on how we as Christians can develop and strengthen our walk of faith. But first, let's explore together the six biblical doors into faith.

THREE

DOOR 1
BE WHO YOU REALLY ARE

Position in Christ

I'd commit suicide . . . ," the frail young woman paused and looked down at her lap, "except I'm not sure I'd go to heaven if I did."

Sarah expelled a long breath and her shoulders drooped. "I was raised in a Christian home and received Christ as a child, but I've never been a very good Christian."

"What do you mean?" I asked.

"I don't read my Bible much. When I try to pray, it seems like nobody is listening. And witnessing!" Her ironic laugh made me shiver, though the day was sunny. "You know that speaker we just heard?"

I nodded.

"He talked about the abundant life we have in Christ. I've been a Christian most of my life, but I have no idea what he's talking about. What have I got to recommend to nonbelievers?"

I had met Sarah a few days before. We were both attending a Christian conference for university students. In other circumstances I might have asked Sarah out. She was tall and slender. Her dark hair accentuated her delicate mouth and large brown eyes. But somehow I had become her "father-confessor" or some kind of counselor, even though I was a new believer myself and we were both about to enter our junior year in college.

"Doesn't the Bible have an answer for people like me?" She looked imploringly at me.

I mentally stumbled around and repeated the few hopeful verses I could remember. But in truth, since I had been a Christian less than a year, I had little more to tell her than the things we had both already heard at the conference.

Sarah's experience is not unusual. Many Christians feel their lives are worthless to God, to others, and even to themselves. Many wonder, *What does God's Word say about people like me?*

Looking back today, I wish I had understood the concept of our position in Christ. I believe if Sarah could have grasped and truly trusted her position in Christ, her whole outlook might have been transformed.

The Real You

To understand the first of our doors into faith, we need to remember the temporary and transitional nature of our current lives. We need to understand how our lives in this "engagement" period are different from what we experienced before we knew Christ. It is also crucial that we know how our lives will change when the "marriage" comes and we are his forever.

The apostle Paul addresses this transitional nature of our current existence when he writes to the Christians in Colossae. "You died, and your life is now hidden with Christ in God" (Col. 3:3 NIV). He also says, "You have been raised with Christ" (v. 1 NIV). What does Paul mean when he says that we as Christians have "died" and "been raised" with Christ?

The moment we receive Christ many things change within us. First, God applies Christ's death and resurrection to us so profoundly that Paul can say we died, were buried, and then were resurrected with Christ. In Romans 6 Paul says, "Don't you know that all of us who were baptized into Christ Jesus were baptized into his death?" (v. 3 NIV). In my own case, the moment I received Christ, I did not feel any different. But Paul is saying that an eternally significant change happened, whether I was aware of it or not. "We were therefore buried with him through baptism into death in order that, just as Christ was raised from the dead through the glory of the Father, we too may live a new life" (v. 4 NIV).

Paul then discusses a second change that happens as a result of our identification with Christ's death. "For we know that our old self was crucified with him so that the body of sin might be done away with, that we should no longer be slaves to sin" (v. 6 NIV). He says, "You have taken off your old self with its practices and have put on the new self, which is being renewed in knowledge in the image of its Creator" (Col. 3:9–10 NIV).

Unfortunately Christian scholars and Bible teachers have not been able to agree on precisely what Paul means when he refers to the "old self" and the "new self."[1] I'm inclined toward the view that the new self is a new capacity for obedience and worship that God supernaturally adds to our soul (the nonphysical part of us) when we receive Christ.[2]

Whatever the new self is, I think one thing is clear. Because of our identification with Christ's death and resurrection, it is now possible for us to live very differently from nonbelievers. After explaining that death no longer has any power over Christ, Paul says,

> In the same way, count yourselves dead to sin but alive to God in Christ Jesus. Therefore do not let sin reign in your mortal body so that you obey its evil desires. Do not offer the parts of your body to sin, as instruments of wickedness, but rather offer yourselves to God, as those who have been brought from death to life; and offer the parts of your body to him as instruments of righteousness.
>
> Romans 6:11–13 NIV

Before we knew Christ, we were "slaves to sin" (v. 17 NIV). We had no choice but to sin. But now we have a choice. When Paul says "count yourselves dead to sin but alive to God," he means that we are to count on it as being true. We are to consider ourselves dead to sin in our thoughts and attitudes and behave as though it were true. Paul tells the Colossians, "Put to death, therefore, whatever belongs to your earthly nature: sexual immorality, impurity, lust, evil desires and greed, which is idolatry" (Col. 3:5 NIV). Instead, he tells them, "clothe yourselves with compassion, kindness, humility, gentleness and patience" (v. 12 NIV).

Let me illustrate what this means by returning to the analogy of engagement. I proposed to my wife, Jan, during Thanksgiving week. She had flown up from college in San Luis Obispo to Portland to spend the week with me. On Sunday afternoon I put her on a plane to return to college.

I remember waking up Monday morning with a strange feeling. I was still in my bachelor apartment. I heard my roommate, Ron, rummaging around in the kitchen, making the same breakfast he made every morning. It seemed like nothing had changed. But in reality much had changed. I had made a commitment that was going to radically affect how I felt, thought, and behaved for the rest of my life.

Later that week, I happened to see a very pretty girl walking through a shopping center. I began to turn my head so I could watch her as she walked by. Then I caught myself. *You're an engaged man! What are you doing gazing at pretty girls in the mall?* I made a conscious choice to turn away and think about Jan. I remembered the entrancing look of shyness and excitement in her eyes as we'd kissed good-bye in the airport. I thought about how fortunate I was to have such a lovely and talented woman agree to marry me. I walked on with love for her in my heart and thoughts of her on my mind. In short, I remembered that I was engaged and chose to allow my heart, mind, and behavior to reflect my true condition.[3]

This is quite similar to what Paul is talking about in Romans and Colossians. When we receive Christ, we bring into our new lives sinful patterns of thought, feeling, and behavior. But now we have a choice. We can choose to consider ourselves as new creations, as those resurrected into new life, and allow our thoughts, feelings, and actions to flow out of what is really true of us. Or we can choose to ignore our new relationship and live as nonbelievers do.

There will come a day when we have our resurrection bodies, when our hearts and minds are fully and finally cleansed from all the old sinful patterns. Then we will be completely free from the pull of the flesh and the world. Then we will be truly one with Christ in our experience. But for now, will we live our "position" in Christ, as we truly are, as those resurrected from the dead, as new creations? Or will we continue to live like the old people we once were, responsive to the lure of the world and to the remnant of our own fallen desires?

One of the first places I learned about my position in Christ was in a little book called *Sit, Walk, Stand,* which was first published in 1957. There, in fewer than eighty pages, Watchman Nee, a leader of the underground church in Communist China, lays out the implications of Paul's teaching in the Book of Ephesians. He organizes the book around three ideas from three key verses. As Christians we are sitting (or seated) with Christ in heaven (Eph. 2:6), we are to walk in a way that is appropriate to that new position (4:1), and we are to stand firmly in that position in times of spiritual struggle (6:11).

Learning to Sit

In Ephesians 2 Paul uses some of the most magnificent language in all of Scripture to explain the benefits God has given us as Christians. He says that God has brought us back to life with Christ "and raised us up with Him, and seated us with Him in the heavenly places, in Christ Jesus" (Eph. 2:6). As Nee explains in the first section of *Sit, Walk, Stand,* we did not do, and could not have done, anything to earn or acquire this lofty position.

Nee asks, "How can we know present deliverance from sin's reign? How is our 'old man,' who has followed us and troubled us for years, to be 'crucified' and put away? Once again the secret is not in walking but in sitting; not in doing but in resting in something done."[4] When we know our position, our first job is just to trust that it is true and rest in it.

I remember vividly when Becky, our firstborn, learned to sit up. She would sit everywhere, on the bed, on the floor, and in her high chair. But what I liked best was when she'd crawl over to where I was sitting, lift her pudgy little arms toward me and say, "Uh, uh" (her version of "up, up"). Then I'd scoop her up onto my lap, she'd snuggle back, and we'd talk or play patty-cake or read one of her picture books.

The important thing to notice is that the high and lofty position (from her perspective) of sitting on Daddy's lap was not something Becky could make happen by herself. She could ask for it but she did not have the ability to climb up into my lap. I had to lift her there and place her there and even hold her there lest she fall. All she needed to do was passively sit.

Through Christ, God has lifted us up and placed us in "his lap." We are seated at his right hand with Christ in the heavenly places, the most honored position in all the universe. God has placed us there through no effort of our own and he is the one who will keep us there.

So the first faith principle to living in our position is to "sit." We need to recognize that God has seated us in a high position of respect and honor. Then we need to simply relax, lean back, and enjoy our position in Christ.

Beginning to Walk

The second section of Watchman Nee's book deals with our faith walk as Christians. Paul urges the Ephesians to "walk in a manner worthy" of their calling as believers (Eph. 4:1). He then goes on to say that we should not walk like unbelievers with minds darkened with sensual impurity (vv. 17–19). Rather we should walk in love as children of light (5:2, 8).

As Nee points out, in Ephesians 4–6 the context of our individual walk is our life in the body of Christ. This is true in two ways. First, relationships with other believers are the places where most of our Christian walk is lived out. But also, when the body of Christ is functioning the way

God intended, it is a great source of encouragement and aid to each of us to walk the way Christ desires.

Even though it was early in my Christian life when I first read the Scripture that compared our Christian lives to physical walking, I don't think I really appreciated the depth of the analogy until I watched my firstborn learn to walk.

Becky was close to a year old when she took her first steps. For weeks she had been walking along holding on to furniture. Sometimes she would stand up, teeter unsteadily in the middle of a room, see something interesting, and take a step or two toward it. Then it seemed as if she realized what she was doing and would quickly drop back to the floor and crawl the rest of the way. Jan and I both felt that she had all the physiological development and skill necessary to walk weeks before she actually took her first conscious, independent steps. It seemed like she had the ability to do it but didn't yet trust it.

Her first real steps came in an unlikely setting, a picnic. We had gone to the park as part of a weekend student-planning retreat. During the two previous days, all the single college women had doted on Becky, the only child present. In every free moment they'd gather around Becky and hold out their hands to her.

"Come on, Becky, let's see you walk!"

She'd take a step and then fall to the floor.

"That's okay. That didn't hurt did it? Get up and try again!"

The girls would help her up. She'd take two steps and then fall.

"That's right. What a big girl! You can do it!"

Each small success was met with cheers, smiles, and praise. Each repeated failure was accepted as normal and spawned renewed encouragement to try again.

Then came the picnic in the park. I remember that the grass was lumpy and uneven. Not a very smooth surface for the steps of a one-year-old. But that was the afternoon when it all came together for little Becky. By the end of the picnic she was toddling all over. Suddenly she believed she could do it. In an afternoon she went from being a crawler to a walker. Of course she still fell regularly. But now no one had to encourage her to get up again. Walking was obviously a superior way to get around.

Since that time I've thought a lot about how the body of Christ influences the individual faith walk of believers. I wonder what would happen to most children if all the adults in their lives ridiculed instead of encouraged them. "What! Are you trying to walk again? Don't you know it's hopeless? Who said you could ever learn to walk?"

And when the kid fell down: "Idiot! Do you know how clumsy you look? Better give up. You'll never make it as a walker!"

If that were the norm, I wonder if any of us would ever learn to walk! But, thankfully, it seems to be an ingrown human instinct to encourage all little kids to take their first steps.

I wish I could say that most churches give the same kind of encouragement to new believers. Wouldn't it be great if every small success were met with ecstatic applause? Wouldn't it be wonderful if temporary failures were greeted with understanding and encouragement? Instead, what happens?

"Oh yes, Julie's enthusiastic about the Lord right now, but you watch; she'll be over that soon enough."

And what will likely happen when somebody notices that Julie has blown it? She's rejected. She's shamed. She gets the message loud and strong. "You're not going to be accepted here if you have problems like that!"

Julie learns that she must look like a good Christian on the outside and not share any of her inner problems, failures, or frustrations. She learns quickly that she'll get no encouragement for real steps of faith and lots of blame for any overt failure. She learns to be a phony.

In Ephesians Paul paints a very different picture of what the church should be like. "Therefore, laying aside falsehood, speak truth, each one of you, with his neighbor, for we are members of one another" (Eph. 4:25). When anyone makes progress, all should rejoice. When anyone falls, all should grieve and try to help him or her up. We are to treat each other "with all humility and gentleness, with patience, showing forebearance to one another in love" (v. 2). But what if a younger Christian (or even an older one) does something that offends us, that really embarrasses us or makes us mad? Paul's answer is clear. "Be kind to one another, tender-hearted, forgiving each other, just as God in Christ also has forgiven you" (v. 32).

Part of the difference between most human families and Christ's body is that the average parent really believes that his child can learn to walk. What if everyone around us in the body of Christ believed in us that way?

So what environment does Paul suggest encourages believers to begin their Christian walk? First, believers need to understand, accept, and rest (sit) in their position, perfect in Christ, seated with him in the heavenlies. Second, they need to be surrounded by an accepting and supportive body of believers who will encourage them in their steps of faith.

But what, exactly, does this practical walk, these steps of faith, look like? Paul tells us to deal with anger right away and not let it grow and fester (vv. 26–27). He encourages every Christian to work hard and not try to get something for nothing (v. 28). We should guard our words so that they build others up, rather than tear them down (v. 29). Our actions and even our words must reflect the highest standards of sexual purity (5:3–5). Husbands and wives should love and honor each other

(vv. 22–33). Children and employees should willingly obey with sincerity those God has placed over them (6:1–3, 5–8). Parents and employers should lead those God has given into their charge, not harshly but firmly yet gently (vv. 4, 9).

Whew! Paul doesn't ask for much, does he? I don't have to look down that list very far to see ways that I have failed in the past and will probably fail again. So what does this mean? Is the Christian walk impractical?

The problem with lists is that we can easily look at them as absolute standards. We can look at our own lives (or those of other Christians) and readily see where we have fallen short.

But I think the right way to look at this list (and other behavioral commands in Scripture) is to see it as a trail God wants us to follow and a description of a destination we will ultimately reach only in the next life. Our Lord does not insist that we arrive the day after we receive him or even fifty years later. He only asks that we begin walking along the path toward becoming the people he wants us to be. And what happens when we fall down or stray off the path? God intends that other believers along the way will reach down and help us up.

Making Our Stand

In the latter portion of Ephesians, Paul speaks about a third aspect of our Christian experience. It centers around the word *stand*. He tells us to "put on the full armor of God, that you may be able to stand firm against the schemes of the devil" (Eph. 6:11). He repeats and expands the thought a few verses later when he says the armor of God will enable us to "resist in the evil day, and having done everything, to stand firm" (v. 13). As Watchman Nee puts it so well: "We must know how to sit with Christ in heavenly places and we must know how to walk worthy of him down here, but we must also know how to stand before the foe."

There came a day, many years after Becky had first learned to walk, when she took a horrible fall and, in fact, Jan and I wondered if she would ever be able to stand (much less walk) again. Jan, Becky, and our son, Rich, were crossing a hump of pavement that separated a sloping driveway from the street. A light snow was starting to fall on that cold February morning. Rich led the way with no difficulty. Becky followed but was surprised by the slippery blacktop. Jan was right behind her and heard the crack as Becky fell with her full weight on her right ankle. There was no doubt it was a serious break. Jan immobilized the leg and rushed Becky to the doctor's office a few minutes away. Even before the anesthetic could take effect, the physician wrenched the foot back around into place and splinted it. (The orthopedic surgeon later said that our doctor's quick action probably saved Becky's foot.) Jan then drove Becky forty-five minutes to the hospital.

In the days following the surgery, Jan stayed with Becky the whole time, even sleeping in the empty ward bed next to Becky's. The physical pain was horrible for Becky, but the emotional pain was probably worse for Jan. At one point Becky even told her she wanted to die. But within a year of the fall, Becky was not only standing but running, jumping, and even ice-skating.

Like Becky, once we have learned to sit and walk, there will come times when we will find it a challenge to even stand up. Our enemy, the devil, loves to sneak up on us and trip us up when we are not expecting it. Some of his challenging temptations are slow and subtle; others are sudden and dramatic, and they take us by surprise.

How should we respond to those who fail to stand, who fall for the devil's schemes, even though they are genuine

Christians? Paul says, "You who are spiritual, restore such a one in a spirit of gentleness; each one looking to yourself, lest you too be tempted" (Gal. 6:1).

What if, when Becky fell, my wife had said, "You clumsy idiot. You've always been the uncoordinated one. You don't see your brother falling like that, do you? I'm embarrassed and disappointed in you. Let me know when you've solved this problem!"

What mother would act like that? No, Jan picked her up in her arms and through her tears did everything she could to see Becky mended.

That's a picture of how we must deal with those in the body of Christ who have failed to stand under the devil's attack. We help them up through our tears. We gently do whatever it takes until they are restored. What it takes may sometimes be as painful as setting a bone without waiting for anesthetic, but we stay right there with the person through it all.

Neil T. Anderson, in books such as *The Bondage Breaker* and *Victory over the Darkness,* links the two ideas that Nee called "sit" and "stand." Anderson says we must know and claim our position in Christ if we are to experience freedom from demonic attack and bondage. Among other prayers, Anderson recommends the following.

> I pray in the name of the Lord Jesus Christ that You, heavenly Father, will rebuke all deceiving spirits by virtue of the shed blood and resurrection of the Lord Jesus Christ. And since by faith I have received You into my life and am now seated with Christ in the heavenlies (Ephesians 2:6), I command all deceiving spirits to depart from me.[5]

Again, Anderson instructs Christian workers, when seeking to help those in demonic bondage, to claim the power of their position:

I take my position with Christ, seated with Him in the heavenlies. Because all authority in heaven and on earth has been given to Him, I now claim that authority over all enemies of the Lord Jesus Christ in and around this room and especially in (name). . . . Now in the name of the Lord Jesus Christ I command you, Satan, and all your hosts to release (name) and remain bound and gagged so that (name) will be able to obey God.[6]

For Anderson, freedom from satanic influence is primarily a matter of knowing and making a decision to believe the truth rather than the lies of the evil one.[7] We are to fill our minds with truths from the Scriptures and choose to believe them. He says that biblical truths (God is loving, merciful, present, available, nurturing, just, and reliable) are filtered through negative life experiences. These experiences might include false teaching, unhealthy relationships, and poor authority role models. When we filter God's truth through this warped grid, God seems unconcerned, unforgiving, critical, rejecting, and untrustworthy. So for Anderson, breaking free from bondage (particularly satanic or demonic) comes primarily from reshaping our thoughts through a series of decisions to believe what we know is true of ourselves and God instead of trusting our feelings or thoughts that have been warped by negative life experiences.

God Is in Control

The Position in Christ door into faith reminds me of a game I once played in a church youth group. (Looking back as an adult, the game now strikes me as rather cruel, though I remember enjoying it as a freshman in high school!)

Our youth leader asked for three volunteers who were then taken to a room in another part of the church. Then the leader briefed the rest of us and had us rehearse exactly what we were supposed to do. Then we sent someone off to get the first victim . . . uh, volunteer.

The first person to return was a nerdy freshman like me. The kid was blindfolded and the leader helped him step up on a hefty two-by-eight board that was slightly off the floor, supported by bricks at each end.

"This is going to be a test of your balance," the youth leader said. "Whichever one of you stays on the board the longest will get a prize."

Then four football players began to lift the board and the freshman off the floor. As instructed they wobbled the board a little and the kid had to flex his knees and wave his arms to keep himself on the board.

"Now be careful; we're gonna take you up a little higher . . ." As the leader continued to speak, he slowly began to bend over, then crouch, until finally his head was right next to the floor. As instructed, the rest of us didn't speak or even move. From everything the freshman's senses were telling him, he was now four or five feet above the floor. But of course he was actually barely higher than where he'd begun.

Suddenly, at the leader's signal, the athletes gave the board a much larger twist, enough to knock the kid off the board. At the same moment the leader yelled, "Look out, don't hit the light!"

As planned, the kid ducked and fell off the board, bracing himself for a dangerous drop of several feet. Instead, he landed flat-footed, having fallen mere inches. The rest of us laughed at his awkwardness and the scared look on his face.

The second volunteer was the junior class treasurer, a pretty blonde. She got an even bigger laugh with her look of embarrassed mortification.

Then the final kid came out. We were all looking forward to this. He was the school brain, equally brilliant in

science, math, and music. I think we all relished the idea
that, for once, somebody would get the best of him.

Everything seemed to be going fine until the youth
leader was down next to the floor and yelled, "Watch out
for the fixture!"

Instead of ducking and falling, the kid simply hopped
off the board, whipped off his blindfold, and laughed at us
and the leader, scrunched down on the floor.

We all just groaned. I never found out how he knew
the board was still next to the floor.

Our experience as Christians in this fallen world is much
like the blindfolded kids on the board. We often find ourselves in situations where all of our senses and our natural instincts (conditioned by our past experiences and the
current lies of the devil) are telling us a distorted version
of life: You can't trust God. He doesn't care about you.
You're a lousy sinner; why should he come through for
someone like you? He's abandoned you—you're on your
own, buddy!

But God and the Bible paint a very different picture:
God loves you and is faithful. You are a child of the King.
You are seated with Christ in the heavenlies. God accepts
you just as you are. He views you as completely righteous
because of Christ. You have the power to conquer any
temptation or trial you face.

So, like the kids, we have to make a decision. We can
say, "It sure sounds and feels like this situation is out of
control. I'd better just duck and prepare myself for the
worst!" Then we end up defeated and humiliated.

Or we can say, "I know that this situation is not as it
seems. I trust that God is in control and I'm in no real danger." Then we have to act on what we know is true, hop
off the board, and get the last laugh on Satan. It is a choice
we will have to make, to a greater or lesser degree, every
day of our lives until we are home with God and sin is no
more.

That is the message I wish I had understood enough to pass along to Sarah thirty years ago. "Your life is not as it appears! It is hidden in Christ. You are seated with him in the heavenlies. You are a princess, a precious and valuable daughter of the King. You can learn to sit and rest in your exalted position. You can gradually learn to walk in a manner worthy of who you really are. And you can find the power to stand against the lies and temptations of the evil one."

It was a message that young woman badly needed to hear. Many in our world today need to have that same message penetrate deep into their hearts and lives.

FOUR

DOOR 2
LET YOUR
PRIDE BE
BROKEN
Death to Self

I walked out of the room stunned. I couldn't believe what I had heard. A man I had known, respected, and admired for many years—a man I wanted to like and respect me—had just reamed me out. He'd told me I was lazy, irresponsible, greedy, wasteful, and a lousy husband and father!

I was certain he could not really mean the things I thought I'd heard. So I went back the next day, asking for clarification. Boy, was that a mistake! He repeated everything from the day before and heaped on a few new accusations. I was so stunned that it was nearly a week before I told my wife what had happened.

The irony of this conversation is that it came at the end of one of the most difficult

years of my life. I had been working hard in the first year
of my doctoral studies and devoting much time and energy
to my aging parents and my children—the accusation of
laziness seemed so unfair as to be ludicrous!

Because I felt close to this man, I couldn't just ignore
his criticisms. As the weeks went by, I slipped deeper and
deeper into depression. I sought the counsel of a pastor
who strongly advised me to back out of as many responsibilities as I could for the next three months. During that
time I wept, I prayed, I read, and I slept. Sometimes I would
wake up so depressed, I could hardly move out of bed.
After three months, I had recovered enough to function.

That was many years ago. Looking back with the rela-
tive objectivity of time and distance, I'm able to answer
several questions that haunted me during my months of
depression.

Were his criticisms literally true as he stated them? No.

Was there a germ of truth in some of them? Yes, that is
partly why they hurt so much.

Did he state his criticisms in a constructive and wise
fashion? Definitely not!

Did God intend something good to come out of the
experience? Without question!

I believe the primary reason God allowed that wrenching experience was to break through my wall of arrogant
self-will and crush my insensitive pride. Over the years I
have come to realize that God has blessed me with many
natural gifts of personality and temperament that are an
asset in Christian service. I have a quick mind. I am generally optimistic, enthusiastic, and adventurous. This pro-
pels me to seek out new ideas and approaches and encourages me to innovate and experiment, even when others
say a task is impractical or impossible. But on the flip side
of these strengths are a series of dangerous weaknesses. I
am often unrealistic, emotional, and unwise in my enthusiasm. I am easily bored and find discipline (whether phys-

ical, mental, or spiritual) difficult and demotivating. I find it very hard to follow through on long, involved projects (like writing a book!). But the worst of these failings is pride. I usually believe my ideas are better than anyone else's. I often respond badly to criticism. When people oppose what I want, too often my response (at least inside) is anger or depression.

The Bible has some strong things to say about pride and those who are proud. James declares, "God is opposed to the proud, but gives grace to the humble" (James 4:6). In the list of destructive things that well up from inside the human, there is pride along with theft, murder, adultery, deceit, envy, and slander! (Mark 7:20–23). Pride, I'm afraid, does not travel in very presentable company. In fact God promises that eventually he will "put an end to the arrogance of the proud" (Isa. 13:11).

Why is pride so roundly condemned in Scripture? Because at its root, pride is idolatry. Pride is a form of self-worship. It is no surprise that it was the primary sin of Satan (Isa. 14:12–14).

We have previously explored the idea that we live in a transition time, similar to engagement. One of the things God is doing with us between the moment we receive Christ and the time we die is maturing us and preparing us for eternity. And what will be one of our primary tasks in eternity? To praise and glorify God forever. This is not a task for the proud. Rather, it is a job for the meek and humble.

Jesus began the Sermon on the Mount by talking about those whom life has crushed. "Blessed are the poor in spirit: for theirs is the kingdom of heaven. Blessed are they that mourn: for they shall be comforted. Blessed are the meek: for they shall inherit the earth" (Matt. 5:3–5 KJV). Later in the sermon Jesus promises, "Blessed are the pure in heart: for they shall see God" (v. 8 KJV).

How does God purify our hearts? How does he turn prideful, self-willed sinners into saints who are humble enough to glorify him as he deserves? I believe that one of his most effective techniques is to use people and circumstances to break down our pride, self-confidence, and self-will.

Cracked Pots

Paul develops this picture of the Christian life rather completely in 2 Corinthians 4. He begins in verse 6 talking about the light of God, which we as Christians have inside of us. "For God, who said, 'Let light shine out of darkness,' made his light shine in our hearts to give us the light of the knowledge of the glory of God in the face of Christ" (2 Cor. 4:6 NIV). He then says that we have this light of God hidden in a very plain sort of container. "But we have this treasure in jars of clay to show that this all-surpassing power is from God and not from us" (v. 7 NIV). Normally in Paul's day, a treasure such as perfume or valuable oil would be kept in a beautiful, decorated vase, not in a cheap clay jar. But here Paul's picture is that God has put the most priceless treasure in the universe, the very life and light of God himself, in plain, nondescript containers—you and me! And how is the life of God released from these plain containers? Paul explains that we, the containers, must be splintered and even broken.

> We are hard pressed on every side, but not crushed; perplexed, but not in despair; persecuted, but not abandoned; struck down, but not destroyed. We always carry around in our body the death of Jesus, so that the life of Jesus may also be revealed in our body. For we who are alive are always being given over to death for Jesus' sake, so that his life may be revealed in our mortal body.
>
> 2 Corinthians 4:8–11 NIV

Paul's picture is of the plain clay jar of our lives being cracked and broken so that the sweet perfume of the life of God may flow freely from us. But, paradoxically, this breaking does not destroy us. It transforms us into vessels that shine with the glory of God. In the midst of the most life-rending experiences, we can see the eternal purpose of God. "Therefore we do not lose heart. Though outwardly we are wasting away, yet inwardly we are being renewed day by day. For our light and momentary troubles are achieving for us an eternal glory that far outweighs them all" (vv. 16–17 NIV).

What exactly did Paul mean by "light and momentary troubles"? Later in 2 Corinthians he tells us that he has experienced more pain and suffering than any Christian leader of his time.

> I have worked much harder, been in prison more frequently, been flogged more severely, and been exposed to death again and again. Five times I received from the Jews the forty lashes minus one. Three times I was beaten with rods, once I was stoned, three times I was shipwrecked, I spent a night and a day in the open sea, I have been constantly on the move. I have been in danger from rivers, in danger from bandits, in danger from my own countrymen, in danger from Gentiles; in danger in the city, in danger in the country, in danger at sea; and in danger from false brothers. I have labored and toiled and have often gone without sleep; I have known hunger and thirst and have often gone without food; I have been cold and naked. Besides everything else, I face daily the pressure of my concern for all the churches. Who is weak, and I do not feel weak? Who is led into sin, and I do not inwardly burn?
>
> 2 Corinthians 11:23–29 NIV

Notice that Paul's catalog of suffering includes examples of physical, mental, emotional, and spiritual pain. And yet he refers to all of this, and anything you and I have suffered, as "light and momentary troubles." Was Paul a masochist? Did he have an unusually high tolerance for pain? I don't think so. I think he was an incredibly gifted but a proud and stubborn man whom God had broken through years of hardship and suffering. And he was also a man who had tasted deeply of the joy and satisfaction of seeing the life of God flow out from him to others.

I want to make an important observation about all that Paul is saying in 2 Corinthians 4. Paul is not talking about an event; he is talking about a process. I wish I could tell you that after I was confronted and went through several months of depression, I never again exhibited ungodly pride and never needed a further experience of broken-ness. If only that were true! But there is still much in me that is proud and arrogant.

In that painful experience, it was as if God took his hammer and swung it hard at my clay jar. The result was that a large crack opened and some of the holy light of God could shine through. But much of the jar that hides the treasure is still intact. God chips away at that crevice daily with his chisel. And every once in a while, he brings back his arm and takes another swing with the hammer.

Do you find this picture of God a little disturbing? I must admit that sometimes I do. I am more comfortable with seeing God as a loving Father who kindly comforts me when I hurt. But it makes me uneasy to think that God himself may be the one who allows or even intends me to experience pain. Let me share with you two concepts that have helped me make peace with a God who sometimes works to break me.

Twisted Love

First, I have learned that I started out with a warped view of what love really is. I grew up in a family where my father often traveled and, when he was in town, worked long hours and then brought more work home at night. My mother, on the other hand, was a stay-at-home mom. Since my only two siblings died when I was young, my mom had lots of time for me and became the primary disciplinarian in the family.[1] My mother's philosophy in child rearing was significantly shaped by the books of pediatrician Dr. Benjamin Spock.[2] She showered me with love and attention, but I cannot recall her ever spanking me, even once. When I was older, she would reason with me about my behavior, and when I disobeyed, she would have me help design a fair punishment (usually some extra work or loss of privilege). I arrived at my teen years with loads of self-confidence but little discipline.

These tendencies were reinforced during my high school and college years. I came of age during the turbulent sixties. The dominant image of "love" during that period was a Haight-Ashbury hippie, puffing a joint, holding up two fingers, and saying, "Peace and love, brother!" I later realized that my generation's concept of love was really just indifference: "You do your thing, I'll do mine, and neither of us will bug each other." Sadly, this distortion has spawned the current generation's idea of "tolerance." Today you are not considered tolerant unless you believe that all viewpoints and lifestyles are equally valid. This has led to the absurd situation where a genuinely loving Christian student on a university campus may be viewed as an intolerant bigot simply because he or she believes in Jesus' words that there is only one way to God (John 14:6).

God's idea of love is far removed from either the Boomer's notion of loving indifference or the Gen-X concept of radically relativistic tolerance. Christ's love is often like that of a skilled surgeon who is not afraid to cut in order to heal. I frequently find myself with the attitude, "That's enough, God. I only want to be a little bit holy!" But being "slightly holy" is an oxymoron, isn't it? God loves us so much that he will not be content until we are as holy as he is holy (1 Peter 1:16). I tend to cry out and say, "I only want to be holy enough to feel good, not enough to actually *be* good!"

I've often heard Philippians 1:6 quoted as a verse of comfort and assurance. "For I am confident of this very thing, that He who began a good work in you will perfect it until the day of Christ Jesus" (Phil. 1:6). But for me, it is sometimes a not-so-welcome promise. It means that God is going to keep working on me until my very last hour here on earth. It means he is more concerned with my character than my comfort. He cares more about my growth than my gratitude. He is more committed to the long-term state of my heart than he is to my temporary happiness.

And why is he so doggedly determined that I continue to grow? Is it because he is some kind of cosmic sadist who takes pleasure in my pain? That notion is as far from the truth as it could possibly be. He won't give up on my progress toward holiness, even at the expense of my pain, precisely because he sees so clearly how much pain my current condition is continually causing me and those around me.

Let's suppose that someone offered you the following bargain: "If you will let me inflict moderate pain on you for the next thirty seconds, I will guarantee that for the next fifty years, you will never experience any pain again. In fact you will experience continual joy and contentment. And I promise there will be no negative side effects of any kind." I suspect, if we really believed it was true, most of us would be glad to take that deal. God has made a similar, but even better, bargain with us. In exchange for a very short period of time (fifty to seventy years) during which we will experience some episodes of "light and momentary troubles," God will give us an endless eternity of unimaginable joy and pleasure. "In Your presence is ful-

ness of joy; in Your right hand there are pleasures forever"
(Ps. 16:11).

So this is the first concept that has helped me accept a
God who seeks to have me broken. I've realized that God's
idea of love is a more genuine one than my warped and
lax twentieth-century concept.

Where Is God When We Hurt?

The second insight that has aided me in understanding
how a loving God might use brokenness is that God is not
the author of pain and suffering.

It was the first time Gabrielle had come to church since
she'd lost her daughter six weeks before. After the service
I walked over to where she was unsteadily standing, holding on to the end of the pew, surrounded by a cluster of
her friends.

"I am so very sorry," I said and gave her a gentle hug.

She looked up at me. It was obvious she'd been crying
during the service.

"I think the hardest thing right now," she said slowly
and with some difficulty, "is to try and understand why
God would let my little Heidi go through so much pain,
only to take her a few days before her third birthday."

Gaby and her husband, Rolf, had married late and tried
for many years to have a child. Finally, little Heidi had
been conceived and her birth was a cause for celebration
throughout the church community. But Heidi had health
problems from the very beginning. After three operations,
each followed by a long convalescence, Heidi contracted
pneumonia and eventually died with Gaby at her bedside.

"Think of all those doctors and nurses in the hospital,"
said one woman. "Many of them heard the gospel for the
first time while Heidi and all of us were there."

"Maybe God is trying to teach you and Rolf something through all this," suggested Fred, a single man in his late twenties.

Gaby looked at him. "Like . . . what?" Her voice caught as she spoke.

Fred looked a little uncomfortable. "I dunno. Maybe longsuffering or compassion for others who are hurting. By the way, where is Rolf? I haven't seen him."

Gaby pulled a tissue from her purse, looked at it, and then back at Fred. "Rolf said he just wasn't ready to come back to church yet. He's taking it really hard. I guess we both are."

Were Gaby's friends right? Did God cause little Heidi to suffer in order to spread the gospel or to teach her parents some kind of spiritual lesson?

The incident with Gaby happened many years ago, when I was still a young believer, just out of college. I didn't know what to tell her and, for a change, kept quiet. But I have since concluded that the kind of advice her friends were giving Gaby was not helpful. In fact I believe they were promoting a subtly flawed view of the nature of God.

Behind their words (and, I've since discovered, behind much Christian advice to those in pain) is an assumption about God's role in the world. Gaby's comforters assumed that when bad things happen (at least when they happen to Christians), God is the one who, for his own reasons, has caused the pain.

I believe the real situation is not as simple as it sounds. Many Christian thinkers, down through the centuries, have distinguished between two aspects of God's will. First, there is the perfect will of God. This is what God would want to have happen in a perfect world without sin. It would be God's perfect will that no angel or human ever sinned. It would be his perfect will that no evil or suffering ever touched any of his children (including his only begotten Son).³ God's perfect world would have no loss or pain or death.

There is another aspect of the will of God, his permissive will. In God's permissive will, he permitted Satan and Adam to rebel against him and fall into sin. In his permissive will, he allows the multitude of consequences of that fall to affect the entire human race, including Christians. In God's permissive will, some things he hates, like the death of a little child, are still allowed to happen. Some might respond to this distinction by saying, "That's just a bunch of semantic nit-picking! What difference does it make if God causes bad things or just 'allows' them? Bad things still happen, and he's still responsible, 'cause he could have stopped them if he wanted to!"

I actually do think the distinction is an important one. Let's take the example of Gaby's little Heidi. Did God kill that little girl? If he did, then we have to search around for some reason why he did it. I think that is what the other Christians around Gaby were trying to do. They were trying to come up with some "good" that was great enough to counterbalance the horror of that precious little girl's suffering and death. But all their attempts rang hollow (certainly to me and I suspect even more so to Gaby).

But what if God did not desire Heidi's death, but only allowed it as one of the many consequences of sin loose in the universe? I think this makes all the difference. Then God is grieving with Gaby, her husband, and her friends. As Jesus wept at the death of his friend Lazarus, God the Holy Sprit grieves with Christians who are suffering "with groans that words cannot express" (Rom. 8:26 NIV).

I have often pondered what I could have said to Gaby if I had known then what I do today. I think I would have said something like this: "God is suffering with you over the pain and death of your lovely little girl. He did not kill her. Horrible diseases killed her. They are a result of the fall and sin in this world. And he hates them and what they do even more than you do.

"But God does not just sympathize with this horrible situation. Even in the midst of this horror, he is already beginning to do some wonderful things. First, he has taken little Heidi in his arms and done for her what you longed to do so many times. He has stopped all her pain, healed everything that was wrong with her little body, and given her joy beyond anything you or I could hope for.

"And he desires to bring healing and joy to you and Rolf once again, as hard as that may be to imagine. But right now you need to know that he is right here grieving with you through all of your pain and loss."

I have come to believe that much of what Christians (and nonbelievers) say to those who are in pain is not really motivated by a desire to comfort them. I think a lot of us, when we are confronted with someone in grief, are very uncomfortable and want to put distance between ourselves and their pain. So we say things that would minimize or invalidate their suffering. We say some version of, "It's better this way." Is this what God really wants us to do? Is this what he himself does?

Paul tells the Roman Christians to "mourn with those who mourn" (Rom. 12:15 NIV). He does not tell them, "When Christians are in pain, shame them, make them feel unspiritual, and encourage them to hide their grief from you!"

I think it is crucial that we view God not as the author of our pain and suffering but as one who grieves with us, comforts us, and works to bring good out of evil. So this is the second idea that has helped me to accept a God who works to see me broken. God is not the author of my pain, although in his permissive will he will often use the pain and suffering in the world for my good. This leads me to a related idea that I think is crucial for us to understand about brokenness.

The Promise of Pain

"Some of you have already experienced a hurt so bad you thought it might kill you." The elderly man's voice boomed through the room filled with college students. "And if you haven't already experienced pain like that, I promise you, eventually you will. Suffering is simply a part of life in this world."

No, he's wrong! I thought to myself. *And it's a completely inappropriate message for a student group.*

I had recently moved into the dorms at San Francisco State College. Auto insurance rates were prohibitive in San Francisco, so I was dependent on public transportation or my feet. Stonestown Presbyterian Church was the only one within walking distance of the campus, so I was there every Sunday morning.

Mr. Henley taught the college Sunday school class. He was a retired widower in his early seventies. I had been a Christian less than a year and had mostly been exposed to an upbeat, optimistic sort of evangelicalism. I had heard lots of messages on God's grace and the abundant life, few on trials or suffering.

So while Mr. Henley spoke, I silently fumed. *You're going to turn these students off,* I thought. *You should be more positive and encouraging.*

But now, more than thirty years later, I'm grateful for Mr. Henley's severe message. I've since watched the struggles of many believers, especially those who've initially entered a life of faith through one of the more "positive" doors (like the Position in Christ door we discussed in the last chapter). For those, pain and suffering often come as a shock and present a temptation to lose their faith. I've even heard some say, "This Christianity stuff doesn't work. Things were supposed to get better, but I've had more problems and challenges since I became a Christian than I ever did before!"

It's true. Jesus does promise the abundant life, but that is not the whole of what he promised his followers. He also promised his disciples they would be hated by the world. "If they persecuted me, they will persecute you also" (John 15:20 NIV). He said, "In this world, you will have trouble." However, he added, "But take heart! I have overcome the world" (John 16:33 NIV). James exhorts us to "Consider it all joy, my brethren, when you encounter various trials" (James 1:2). Notice James does not say *if* you encounter trials. He says *when*. Mr. Henley was right. All of us who follow Christ will encounter trials, trouble, and even persecution. We need to be prepared to meet them with the insight and perseverance God has provided for us.

The Broken and the Proud

So all believers eventually experience pain and suffering. But I do not think that all hurt serves as a door into faith.

Consider the example of Michelle. Her father was an alcoholic who beat and sexually abused her. Michelle's mother covered for him. She would call his work and tell them he was sick when actually he was too hungover to function. She warned the children never to tell an outsider what their father did lest they be taken from the home and put in some horrible state institution.

Michelle became pregnant at fifteen and ran away with the child's father, a man of twenty-three. Soon it was clear that this man was much like Michelle's own father. He abused drugs, gambled, and slapped her when she even hinted he ought to get a steady job. Eventually, in fear for her child, Michelle found her way to a shelter for abused women. It was there that Michelle first heard about God's love and eventually accepted Christ as her Savior. As a new believer Michelle was fearful, suspicious of men (and anyone in authority), and found it very difficult to trust God.

What is the key to Michelle's spiritual walk? Does she need to experience brokenness to trust God? Unlikely. Life has already broken Michelle. Probably she would respond best to the Position in Christ door, the Living by Grace door, or the Spirit Filled door.

Notice that Paul tells Christian leaders to deal differently with different kinds of believers. In dealing with "rebellious people," he tells Titus to "rebuke them sharply, so that they will be sound in the faith" (Titus 1:10, 13 NIV). But when it comes to those who are already broken, he says, "encourage the timid, help the weak" (1 Thess. 5:14 NIV). So while every Christian will experience brokenness and pain sometime in their lives, brokenness does not serve everyone as a door into faith.

The brokenness door into faith seemed to be a favorite with Christians (and Christian authors) of the Builder generation (people born before the end of World War II). Some of the popular and influential Christian books from this generation include *Born Crucified: The Cross in the Life of the Believer* by L. E. Maxwell[4] (published in the 1940s), *The Calvary Road* by Roy Hession[5] (first published in the 1950s), and the booklet "Continuous Revival" by Norman Grubb[6] (first published in the early 1960s). Watchman Nee also wrote a popular book devoted to the brokenness door, *The Release of the Spirit,* which was first published in 1965 but was undoubtedly based on talks given by Nee many years earlier in China.[7]

It's intriguing to note that this door into faith has largely been overlooked or avoided by my own generation of Christian writers, the Baby Boomers (those born between the end of World War II and the early '60s). The majority of the books on the Christian life in the last thirty years have focused on the more positive doors. There may be a cultural explanation for this shift. The Builder generation of Christians lived through two world wars and the Great Depression. It makes sense that they would feel the need to see how God works through pain and suffering. In contrast, my generation has never known a worldwide war and generally has lived in a stable and healthy economy (at least in North America).

What fascinates me is that the next generation of American Christians (Generation X or Baby Busters) shows signs of reembracing the brokenness door in a big way. While the younger generation of leaders has not yet produced many books (the oldest are still in their thirties), the brokenness door is being taught through popular Christian music.

Leading this resurgence of brokenness as a means to Christian growth is the contemporary recording group Jars of Clay (named for a central brokenness passage, 2 Cor. 4:7). In 1995 their first album, *Jars of Clay*, which went double-platinum and was nominated for a Grammy award, included several songs with a brokenness theme. One example is "Worlds Apart," which features the refrain:

Can I be the one to sacrifice
Or grip the spear and watch the blood and water flow?
To love you—take my world apart
To need you—I am on my knees
To love you—take my world apart
To need you—broken on my knees.[8]

The follow-up CD, *Much Afraid,* which won a Grammy award in 1997, continued the brokenness theme. One of the tracks, "Frail," says in part:

Exposed beyond the shadows,
You take the cup from me.
Your dirt removed my blindness
Your pain becomes my peace.

And then the chorus says:

> If I was not so weak
> If I was not so cold
> If I was not so scared of being broken
> Growing old
> I would be
> I would be
> Frail.[9]

Other contemporary Christian artists and groups seem to be following the lead of Jars of Clay in emphasizing the brokenness door. They include: Smalltown Poets ("Listen Closely," 1998); Satellite Soul ("Great Big Universe," 1999); and Caedmon's Call ("40 Acres," 1999).

I can only wonder if the current generation's experience of broken homes, sexual abuse, and widespread belief that their lives will be worse than those of their parents has led them to a new tenderness and sensitivity to a theology of brokenness.

Mixed Signals

I feel I should tell you that, honestly, I don't like this door very much. (I suppose you may have already figured that out from the great lengths I went to defend it!) There is an odd irony I've noticed about the doors. Sometimes the ones we are least naturally attracted to are the ones we need the most.

The first door we considered, Your Position in Christ door, is definitely one of my "natural" doors. I heard talks about it early in my Christian life, and it just seemed right to me. I'm not sure but I suspect that one of the reasons it felt so right was the warm and close relationship I had with my mom growing up. We spent a lot of time together.

If I wanted her for something, she'd always stop what she was doing and give me her full attention. She gave me the gift of genuine unconditional love. I didn't realize until I was well into adulthood how unusual an experience that was for a kid growing up in the fifties and sixties.

Can you see why it was not so difficult emotionally for me to grasp that I was a "child of the King"? It was not such a stretch for me to imagine that God saw me as positionally perfect. Thanks to my mom, I'd always felt good about myself.

But when it came to brokenness, that was another story. I remember being given some of the classic, Builder generation books on brokenness when I was a young Christian. I dutifully started reading each of them. But I'm not sure I ever made it all the way through, even any of the shorter ones. They were what my generation called "downers" or "bummers." I simply wasn't ready for and didn't see the value of anything negative about Christianity in those days.

But funny thing! It's amazing how life has a way of changing your perspective. Two car accident injuries, several poor professional judgments, and some real bad mistakes in my personal life have left me a lot more sympathetic to learning about brokenness.

There is something odd about the way my orientation and that of my wife, Jan, can warp our ability to appreciate, and sometimes even hear, an emphasis that is foreign to us. Like many couples, Jan and I are opposites. I tend to be a cheery optimist. She's a wary pessimist, oops, I mean realist.

When we read a Scripture passage together, or sit through a sermon, the results are almost unbelievable. I can listen to a sermon and go away feeling quite affirmed and encouraged with maybe just a touch of admonishment thrown in for spice. Jan can sit through the exact same sermon and feel as if she's been flogged for forty minutes.

It also happens when we read the Bible. If we're reading together in Philippians, we might both read the same words: "Work out your salvation with fear and trembling; for it is God who is at work in you, both to will and to work for His good pleasure" (Phil. 2:12–13). But the messages we'd get could be quite divergent. Jan would hear, "God is to be feared and will hold you accountable for your work." I might hear, "Don't sweat it; God is the one responsible for what you accomplish." Who is right? The answer is we're both right and we're both wrong. What each of us received was an incomplete message. In fact it's almost like we got our wires crossed and each received the other's message. What I probably should have heard from that passage was, "Alan, Christ saved you at great expense and you need to take the responsibility that comes with that salvation far more seriously than you do." On the other hand, here's the message the Holy Spirit likely wanted to send to Jan. "My darling daughter, you can relax and rest in me. I have more than enough power to both motivate you and accomplish all I desire in and through you."

Most of the time I would benefit from a swift kick in the pants and Jan needs God's gentle, loving touch.

My point is this. I've learned (the hard way) that the brokenness door, while always unpleasant, is one of the most beneficial for me, precisely because it does not come as naturally as some of the others.

When Jesus says to each of us that we should deny ourselves, take up our cross, and follow him, he is inviting us into a life of brokenness (Mark 8:34). Paradoxically this pain-filled journey is also a joyful pilgrimage of becoming more like Christ himself.

FIVE

DOOR 3
OPEN
YOURSELF
TO LOVE
Under Grace

I sat on the grass that sloped down to the River Cherwell in Oxford, England. I opened my journal, but tears were making it hard to write.

"I can hardly believe that God has been so kind to me," I wrote. "He has truly given me the desire of my heart."

It had been only days after I'd received Christ at age nineteen that I'd first read *The Great Divorce* by C. S. Lewis. Over the years since, his writing had spoken to me, stretched my mind, and ignited my imagination like that of no other author. And now here I was in Oxford where Lewis had spent most of his adult life. I looked up at Magdalen Tower and the window of the bachelor rooms where Lewis had written *Miracles* and *The Chronicles of Narnia*. This visit was the fulfillment of a decades-old dream and the closest I would likely ever come to a pilgrimage.

I'd stopped in England on my way back from teaching a series of classes to missionaries in South Africa. As I sat on the lawn thanking God, a thought entered my head. *Perhaps this is God's way of rewarding me for serving him in South Africa.*

Immediately came the inaudible voice I knew was the Holy Spirit. "This vacation is not something you've earned. I've given it to you simply because I love you!"

Then the tears flowed so hard I gave up all thought of writing in my journal.

The Galatian Snare

It goes against some of our deepest instincts to believe that God gives good things, not because we have earned or deserve them but simply out of the overflow of his grace. Even many of us who are Protestant evangelicals steeped in the Reformation tradition that there is nothing we can do to earn our salvation fall into this trap. We know that we could not merit salvation, but we think we must live the Christian life by working daily to earn God's favor.

Apparently the early Christians in the church at Galatia made this same mistake. The apostle Paul chides them. "Have you lost your senses? After starting your Christian lives in the Spirit, why are you now trying to become perfect in your own human effort?" (Gal. 3:3 NLT). They had begun their Christian lives by admitting they could not keep God's standards and trusting the Holy Spirit to give them a new nature. But now they believed it was up to their own efforts to become better Christians and do the things that would please God.

I think the reason God's grace is hard for us to trust at an emotional level is that it runs so contrary to every other relationship in our lives. Our coworkers, our friends, our teachers, and even our closest family members tend to react to our behavior. When we do what they want, when we are pleasant and friendly and enjoyable to be around, we experience their approval and love. But when we disappoint them, when we embarrass or hurt them, their reactions to us are quite different. It is understandable that at some deep emotional level we might expect God to treat us the same way everyone else does. I think it is a perfectly normal human response, conditioned by nearly all of our life experiences, to expect God to bless and reward us when we perform as he desires and to withhold his blessing, or even punish us, when we disappoint or disobey him.

Evangelical Superstition

Most American Christians are quick to reject some of the more obvious forms of superstition. Most of us do not throw salt over our shoulders, avoid walking under ladders, or think that a broken mirror will bring us seven years of bad luck. I remember being astonished when I first visited Russia to find how widespread many superstitions were, even among the highly educated.

Nadia was a Russian public schoolteacher in her mid-thirties, a single mom with a twelve-year-old son who was in poor health. She was earning a little extra by serving as one of the interpreters for our group of Western Christians. One evening in St. Petersburg, Udo Middleman[1] and I decided we'd like to take a stroll along the canals and find a coffeehouse for a little snack before bed. We asked Nadia along to interpret for us. (Between us we may have known five words of Russian!) We finally found a place that would serve us some bread and tea. As we slid into a typical Russian high-backed rectangular booth, Nadia protested.

"Oh, no, I mustn't sit at the corner. If I do, I'll never get married again."

Later we suggested that the waiter take a photo of the three of us.

"No," said Nadia. "Everyone who's ever appeared with me in a picture has either died or I've lost them as a friend. I don't want to lose either of you!"

It was easy for Udo and me to see the sad foolishness of Nadia's superstitions, and we spent the next hour sharing with her how she could be freed from her fears through Jesus Christ. But we American evangelicals have superstitions that probably look just as foolish to God but are much harder for us to detect.

We are sometimes tempted to view God's blessing as a kind of perk or reward for good behavior, just as I did by the river in Oxford. And when bad things happen, we wonder what misdeed or error God is punishing. See if any of these thoughts sound familiar: *That car accident today. Was that because I didn't have my quiet time? Or how about that misunderstanding at work? Is that because I skipped church on Sunday?*

Wait a minute, you may be thinking. *Doesn't the Bible say, "God is not mocked; whatever a man sows, he also reaps"?*

Yes, the Bible does say that (in Galatians 6:7). It is a general principle, expressed in many passages of Scripture, that there is a natural cause and effect, not only in the physical world but also in the mental, emotional, and spiritual realms. Sometimes bad things in our lives can be traced to our own neglect or lack of discipline. But these verses are not talking about what I'm calling "evangelical superstition."

Let me try to clarify the difference with a hypothetical example. Let's suppose I'm caught for an hour in slow traffic. Each time a driver cuts in front of me, I get angrier and angrier. Finally, I've had it. Another guy's about to cut in, so I gun the engine to close up the gap. Unfortunately, the lady in front of me chooses that exact moment to slam on her brakes, and the front of my car collapses into her taillights.

Could there be a connection between that accident and my missed quiet time that morning? Perhaps. Maybe if I'd spent twenty minutes that morning meditating on John 14:27,[2] I'd have found it easier to control my road rage. But if that connection does exist, it is the sort of emotional and spiritual cause and effect Paul is talking about in Galatians. God is not *punishing* me for missing my quiet time. The missed quiet time was merely a contributing factor to my being ill prepared to effectively handle the stress of my day.

But now let's suppose I'm driving along at a safe distance behind the car in front. I'm not angry. I'm not impatient. I'm just following the flow of traffic. Suddenly the lady in front of me slams on her brakes. I hit mine and am able to stop my car a few inches from her bumper. Suddenly a large truck plows into my rear end at 20 miles per hour. Ten minutes later, as the police try to pry open my crumpled door, I wonder, *Maybe this happened because I missed my quiet time this morning.* That would be evangelical superstition.

"Reaping what we sow" is when we receive the natural consequences (or benefits) that God has built into the way our universe naturally works. "Evangelical superstition" is when we think God is punishing (or rewarding) us for our performance even when there is no normal or reasonable connection between what we've done and what we've received afterward.

Not under the Law

There is a section of the New Testament that is (in my experience) poorly understood by most Christians. And even those who do understand it with their heads often fail to practice what they know with any consistency in their lives. I'm talking about Paul's extended discussion of law and grace, which begins in Romans 5:20 and continues all the way to Romans 8:4. Buried in the middle of this discussion is the profound proclamation, "Sin shall not be master over you, for you are not under law, but under grace" (6:14).

But what does it mean to be under grace? Let me begin by clearing up a fairly minor but potentially damaging misconception. I've sometimes heard Christians say to each other, "You're putting me under the law" or "You need to learn to live under grace, not under the law." The error here is somewhat subtle. If we truly know Christ, it is impossible for someone to put us under the law. We do not have to make a choice between living under the law and living under grace. Paul makes it clear to the Romans that they are not under the law; rather, they are under grace. Neither you nor anyone else can ever put you back under the law. You were liberated from the restrictions and penalties of the law the moment you received Christ. Whether you understand it, whether you believe it, whether you even wish it—you are under grace!

Wait a minute, you may be thinking, *do you mean I have no choice to make about grace in my day-to-day Christian life?* The answer to that question is yes, you do have a choice to make.

But the choice is not whether to live under the law or under grace. Your choice is whether you will believe you are under grace and live your life in a manner that is consistent with your belief. There is a parallel between your decision with regard to grace and what we learned in the chapter on our position in Christ. There we learned that we have to begin by accepting and believing what the Bible says is true about us. We must first believe that we are seated in the heavenlies with Christ Jesus. Then we can walk in a worthy manner and stand in times of trial.

In a similar fashion, we must believe that we really are no longer under the law. One of the themes of this book is that our Christian life is a transition period, similar to engagement. First, we must realize that we are no longer single, independent, autonomous. Our lives, our time, our treasure, our emotions do not simply belong to us as they once did. We are now engaged. Our lives are centered more and more on our fiancé. Our family life, our priorities, how we spend our time—all of these are changing in light of this new reality.

Often engagement is followed by a period of wondering disbelief. I have often heard the newly engaged say, "I can't believe she said yes." Or "I can't believe he finally got up the nerve to actually propose." I think that's part of the reason for things like an engagement ring, an engagement party, wedding showers. These are tangible ways to reinforce to the couple, and everyone around them, that this engagement is real—a wedding is really going to happen.

Likewise, we as believers need to realize, at a profound emotional level, that our relationship with God has changed. He has accepted us unconditionally. Like the prodigal son, our Father's love for us is guaranteed; we don't have to do anything to earn it.

Free from the Tutor

There is a subtle and beautiful picture of what the law can, and cannot, accomplish in our lives found in Galatians 3:23–4:7. In this passage, Paul compares the law to a tutor. "Therefore the Law has become our tutor to lead us to Christ, that we may be justified by faith. But now that faith has come, we are no longer under a tutor" (Gal. 3:24–25). Paul is not talking here about what we generally mean by the word *tutor* today. This was not an expert teacher, hired to give private remedial work to a student having problems with math or English. The Greek word Paul uses in this passage is *paidagogos*. In the Greco-Roman world, the *paidagogos* was usually a slave assigned by a wealthy landowner to make sure the firstborn son received an education.[3] The slave was not the child's teacher but more of a disciplinarian who made sure the son and heir got to school, paid attention, and did his homework. The slave generally had the responsibility of corporal punishment and could beat the child if he got up late, played hooky, fell asleep in class, or failed to finish his assignments. No wonder Paul goes on to say "as long as the heir is a child, he does not differ at all from a slave although he is the owner of everything."

Why was the firstborn son treated so badly? It was not because the father hated him and wanted his son's life to be miserable. Quite the opposite. Often the oldest son was the only offspring who had the privilege of receiving the finest education.[4] The reason for the severe discipline of the tutor was so the son would learn all he needed to by the date set by the father. For on that day, the son would inherit everything. He would become responsible for all the land, the household, and all the servants, including the tutor.

Since I suspect boys have been much the same in every age, I imagine more than one Roman heir had daydreams of revenge on his tutors. *Just wait 'til graduation day,* little Andronicus—Andy—thinks to himself. *I'm going to give that nasty tutor a beating far worse than he ever gave me!* But the imagined revenge was probably rare. You see, one of the subjects Andy would be learning was the proper care and management of servants. By graduation day, Andy would realize that his tutor was one of his most precious and valuable resources. He would also be mature enough to grasp that the tutor had not punished him out of any personal hatred but for his own good.

Let's imagine, for a moment, the morning after graduation. Andy sleeps in a little, since the tutor is not there to wake him up. Andy steps out of his room and sees his former tutor coming down the hall. Andy flinches at the sight of him, remembering all the beatings he's received for oversleeping. But this morning things are different. The servant comes up to Andy, bows low, and says, "Good morning, master, how may I serve you today?"

How does all this apply to us? All of us, male or female, young or old, are like the firstborn son and heir. We too have a tutor, which is the law. Paul says the law is our tutor to lead us to accept Christ and receive justification by faith. How does the law do that? It does it by showing us our sinfulness. When we sincerely do our best to keep the Old Testament law (or Jesus' Sermon on the Mount or Paul's moral exhortations in his letters), we soon realize that we will never keep it perfectly. In fact James compares the law (and the entire Word of God) to a mirror (James 1:23–25). We look into the mirror of the law and we can see by how far we fail to measure up to its standard. As one old preacher put it, "Many folks aren't ready to accept Christ until they've spent some time in law school!" The law, Paul says, was designed to show us how sinful we are and persuade us that we need a redeemer. But the law does not have any power to make us holy (Rom. 8:3; 3:20; Gal. 2:16). When we understand we cannot be good enough on our own, then the law has finished its work. We are now ready to accept Christ by grace through faith. From the very moment we accept him, we are no longer under our tutor, the law. Does this mean we ignore the law, that we abuse or misuse it? Does this mean we go out and engage in every sort of sin with impunity? If we have truly "graduated," if the law has truly taught us how sinful we are, then we won't desire to break God's law any more than the mature son and heir would take his vengeance on the tutor. The Christian should desire to behave in a manner that is holy and honoring to God.

Three Law Keepers

Wait a minute, you may be thinking. *If a Christian who is saved by grace still honors and keeps the law, then what has changed?* It's an excellent question. What has changed is the believer's attitude toward the law. Christians should not keep the law out of fear or in an attempt to earn God's favor. Rather, they do what the law says because they know it is in their own enlightened self-interest and because they know it pleases and honors the God who has freely and unconditionally saved them.

This is one of the trickiest and most potentially deceptive parts of our Christian life. There are three groups of people who, on the outside, may look a lot alike. The first group is made up of the moral, religious, nonbelievers who think they can be saved by living moral lives. These are the unsaved legalists. In the second group are the genuine believers who think they have to keep the law to please God and earn his favor. These are the saved legalists. In the third group are the genuine believers who understand they are under grace and live morally because they know it's the best way to live and are grateful to the God who freely saved them. These are the saved, living in the light of grace. The behavior of people in the three groups may be identical. The only difference you may be able to detect is that the believers who know they are under grace will likely demonstrate a joy and freedom those in other groups do not experience.

"I can't believe you signed it!" Matt looked like he'd just seen a specter. "Why, that's legalism. I'm quite surprised you're giving in to it."

Matt had just invited Jan and me for a round of pinochle at his house. I'd had to break the news that it would be another four months before we could say yes to the proposed game. I'd taken a semester adjunct faculty position at a local Christian college. All the faculty were required to sign a statement promising not to drink, smoke, play cards, and a few other things as long as we were teaching there. The pinochle was the only thing on the list I'd miss.

"I'm not giving in to anything," I said. "I just decided that teaching would be a great ministry and good experience—and this restriction goes with the territory."

"Yeah, but what about your freedom in Christ?" Matt asked. "You need to throw off this yoke of slavery and stand up for the gospel of grace!"

"I'm not sure this has anything to do with the gospel," I said. "I'm just going to teach and not play cards for a semester. That's all."

Matt shook his head. "I don't think in good conscience I could do that."

Was Matt right? Was I submitting myself to a legalistic system by signing the agreement?

Not at all. In fact it was exactly the opposite. It was specifically because I knew I was under grace that I could in good conscience sign the paper. I knew I had the freedom to play cards under God's grace. I was temporarily giving up this small freedom for the sake of what I believed would be a significant ministry. I was not doing it to curry favor with the school administration. I certainly was not doing it to earn God's favor. It was for the ministry. Period. And when the semester was over, we had a big party and invited Matt and his wife over for (you guessed it) an evening of pinochle.

The regulations at the Christian school illustrate my point about three groups that look alike. I have no doubt that at the college there were Christian kids who were keeping the rules to please their parents or the administrator or even God. These would be the saved legalists. There were also a number of nonbelievers present on the campus (mostly there for athletics). So it's conceivable there were a few legalists of the unsaved variety too.

So we had the strange situation of all the students and the faculty signing the exact same document. But for some the document was legalistic and for others, like me, it was just a minor inconvenience. What made the difference? Attitude. We all behaved in the same way (defined by what we were not doing). But for some it was legalism because they were obeying not in faith but under compulsion. However, for others, obeying the rules was an act of faith.

Law School

Let me illustrate how the law functions as a tutor through the true story of my friend Rex. Rex had always been very musical as a kid and by the time he reached high school, he was active in choir and various school musical productions. Then a group called Moral Re-Armament (MRA) showed up in Rex's town with a program called Up With People.[5] Rex excitedly joined the local youth touring group and began singing in the Up with People musical productions. One of the first things the Moral Re-Armament staff encouraged Rex to do was to take the MRA pledge to the Four Absolutes: absolute purity, absolute unselfishness, absolute honesty, and absolute love. Rex enthusiastically took the pledge and jumped with great energy into living his new moral life. However, Rex soon discovered his purity was severely challenged by sexual thoughts, he often acted selfishly, he found it difficult to tell the truth in everything, and he was far less loving than he'd ever realized. By the end of the first week, Rex felt like a total failure and was quite discouraged. After choir practice that Friday, the high school music director called Rex into his office and closed the door.

"Rex, I couldn't help noticing the hangdog face. Is something wrong?"

Rex proceeded to blurt out the whole story in a single breath.

"I see," said the director. "Well I have some good news for you."

With that the choir director shared the gospel with Rex and invited him to receive Christ.

"I was so ready," Rex later told me. "After a week of trying my best to keep the Four Absolutes, I knew I was a hopeless sinner and needed a Savior."

For Rex the teachings of Moral Re-Armament functioned like the law and became a tutor to prepare him for Christ's message of forgiveness. It took Rex only one week in "law school" before he was ready to graduate.

Unfortunately, it is not only nonbelievers who occupy seats in law school. Many Christians are living like the Galatians. Even though they are no longer under the law, they are still trying to live as if they were. Pastor Steve McVey was one such Christian. In his book *Grace Rules,* he tells that for twenty years of ministry his focus was on his own behavior and service to God.

> I believed that Christians were saved to serve, and I certainly wanted to fulfill the purpose of my salvation. So I dedicated myself to serving Jesus. I was diligent and sincere and often felt successful at it. With my Bible in one hand and my Day Timer in the other, I went forward to make my mark for God in this heathen world. . . . I did notice that no matter how much I did for Jesus, I felt an inner "To Do List" hanging over my head.[6]

Eventually McVey made a startling discovery; God does not need our service! Instead he was shocked to learn that God wants *us* and a relationship with us.

> When the concept of our relationship to God is service-oriented, we will relate to Him as a divine Employer who scrutinizes our activity to make sure it is up to standard. Our focus will be on our performance as we attempt to do the things we believe He requires. This mindset reflects a legalistic view of the Christian life, a view that's erroneous. God doesn't want us to focus on our service to Him. When grace rules our lives, we focus on Him. In doing so, we experience intimacy in such a way that service becomes a natural overflow of the love relationship.[7]

Yet legalism is a subtle and deceptive force that can creep into our lives and churches and stifle the freedom that God wants us to experience in our relationship with him. Chuck Swindoll writes:

> I find it more than strange. Actually, I find it amazing that we as a nation will fight other nations for our national liberty, and that we as a people will, if necessary, fight one another for the freedom of those within our borders, but when it comes to the living out of our Christianity, we will give up our liberty without a fight. We'll go to the wall and square off against any enemy who threatens to take away our national freedom, but we'll not be nearly so passionate as Christians under grace to fight for our rightful liberty. Let enough legalists come aboard and we will virtually give them command of the ship. We will fear their frowns, we will adapt our lives to their lists, we'll allow ourselves to be intimidated, and for the sake of peace at any price (even though it may lead to nothing short of slavery), we will succumb to their agenda.[8]

In his wonderful book *What's So Amazing about Grace?* Philip Yancey writes about his own legalistic upbringing

in fundamentalism and the many years it took him to overcome its effects and find a genuine relationship with the
God of grace. Yancey also tells the tragic story of his own
brother, who for the past thirty years "has tried to escape
that ironclad moralism—and so far has succeeded in escap-
ing God as well."[9]

Yancey concludes his discussion of legalism with the following telling analogy.

> I once read that proportionally the surface of the earth is
> smoother than a billiard ball. The heights of Mount Ever-
> est and the troughs of the Pacific Ocean are very impres-
> sive to those of us who live on this planet. But from the
> view of Andromeda, or even Mars, those differences mat-
> ter not at all. That is how I now see the petty behavioral
> differences between one Christian group and another.
> Compared to a holy and perfect God, the loftiest Everest
> of rules amounts to a molehill. You cannot earn God's
> acceptance by climbing; you must receive it as a gift.
>
> Jesus proclaimed unmistakably that God's law is so per-
> fect and absolute that no one can achieve righteousness.
> Yet God's grace is so great that we do not have to. By striv-
> ing to prove how much they deserve God's love, legalists
> miss the whole point of the gospel, that it is a gift from God
> to people who don't deserve it. The solution to sin is not
> to impose an ever-stricter code of behavior. It is to know
> God.[10]

Beyond Fair

Perhaps the most powerful picture of legalism in Scripture comes at the very end of Jesus' story of the prodigal
son. You remember the story. A wealthy man's younger
son demands his share of the family fortune, then wastes
it in high living. When he returns repentant, the father

rejoices and throws a celebration feast. But do you remember how the story ends?

> The older brother was angry and wouldn't go in. His father came out and begged him, but he replied, "All these years I've worked hard for you and never once refused to do a single thing you told me to. And in all that time you never gave me even one young goat for a feast with my friends. Yet when this son of yours comes back after squandering your money on prostitutes, you celebrate by killing the finest calf we have."
>
> Luke 15:28–30 NLT

From one point of view, the older son had a good reason to complain, didn't he? If the issue was fairness or equality of treatment, then the father was not really being fair, was he? The older son's basic complaint was, "My brother doesn't deserve this feast." And that's right; he didn't deserve it, did he? Grace always speeds past plodding ideas like fairness, justice, and equality. Grace knows only the turbocharged and reckless abandon of extravagance.

Here's the father's reply: "Look, dear son, you and I are very close, and everything I have is yours. We had to celebrate this happy day. For your brother was dead and has come back to life! He was lost, but now he is found!" (Luke 15:31–32 NLT). The father's focus was on the restored relationship, not on whether each son was the same or received the same.

A number of years ago, when all three of our children were still living at home, our oldest daughter, Becky, needed a car to drive to school. At that time she had a good, steady job and could, we felt, pay her own expenses on a car. So we offered to sell her our old Subaru at well below the Blue Book value. Becky had no problem with this arrangement until a few years later when her younger brother also needed a car. He was not working, and we chose to give him the old van we no longer needed. Becky came to me privately, and I could see she was deeply grieved.

"When I needed a car, you made me buy it from you but now you've given him one free." Then she uttered the words every parent learns to dread. "It just doesn't seem fair!"

I told her that our desire was to give each of our children what we felt they needed and what would be good for them out of the resources we had available at the time. I told her that what we had done for her and for her brother was motivated out of love for them, not primarily out of a sense that we had to be fair or help each of them exactly the same.

Becky was still not satisfied, so I took her to Jesus' parable of the laborers in the vineyard. She did not seem to have ever seen the story before. We read together how a landowner hired some men at dawn to work in his vineyard for the standard daily wage. Later he hired some more men at nine o'clock and later more at noon. Finally, he hired some more men at five in the afternoon. At six o'clock he called all the men in and gave them all the same day's wages. Becky and I read how the ones who'd worked since dawn complained. "Those people worked only one hour, and yet you've paid them just as much as you paid us who worked all day in the scorching heat" (Matt. 20:12 NLT).

Becky looked up at me. "It doesn't seem fair. How can Jesus teach this example when it isn't fair?"

Then we read the landowner's answer to one of the workmen. "Friend, I haven't been unfair! Didn't you agree to work all day for the usual wage? . . . Should you be angry because I am kind?" (vv. 13, 15 NLT).

I'm not sure Becky really grasped the point of what I was trying to tell her until years later when the old Subaru was falling apart. That fall her grandmother and her parents made it possible for her to buy a brand-new car to take to graduate school.

Like our love for our daughter, God's gracious love for us is not about fairness or equality. It's about relationship. God loves all his children with the same infinite quality of love. But his relationship with each of his children is unique, because he's made each one of us unique.

Legalistic Christians expect praise for swimming against the current of the world to keep God's rules. Grace-filled Christians know they are hopeless sinners kept afloat by the rushing torrent of God's grace.

SIX

DOOR 4
LET CHRIST
LIVE
THROUGH
YOU
Exchanged Life

I'd lost my keys again! Sometimes I really do deserve the title "absentminded professor." But this time I was late for an important meeting, Jan was gone (and with our only other set of car keys), and I was really beginning to feel idiotic (and more than a little concerned!).

"Slow down, Alan," I told myself. What was it my mother taught me so many years ago? I could still hear her voice echoing in my thoughts.

"When you lose something, slow down and go back and look everywhere again, more methodically this time."

So I went back to the bedroom. Not on the top of the nightstand where I always leave them. How about in the drawers? This

time I moved everything around, and even took the big
stuff out, in case the keys were underneath or behind. Still
no luck. Maybe they fell and got kicked under the dresser
or under the bed. This time I got a flashlight and checked
slowly and thoroughly. Nothing.

I expanded the search to the bathroom and the kitchen
with the same methodical attention. Now I was really late
and my level of frustration was growing. It was getting
harder and harder to search slowly and carefully.

Then it hit me. I hadn't even prayed about the keys.
"Oh, Lord," I said, "I can't believe I've left you out of this!
You're not upset or in a hurry, are you? I'll just stop trying and let Christ take over. I'll relax and get out of the
way. If you want me at the meeting, you'll need to find
the keys and get me there."

Immediately I had this delightful sense of all the anxiety and tension flowing out of me, like stuffy air from a
hot room when the door is opened in winter. And I felt
the cool breath of Christ's Spirit soothing my mind and
heart. And then the thought came, quietly and easily: *You
wore the green jacket yesterday.*

I walked the few paces to the coatrack behind the big
recliner, quite certain of what I'd find. The keys were in
the pocket.[1]

I've had similar experiences throughout my Christian
life. In fact, just this morning, after pondering for some
time how to start this chapter, I was beginning to be concerned that I couldn't think of an appropriate example.
Suddenly I realized I hadn't specifically prayed about it! I
don't think my prayer even took the form of words. I just
mentally switched my focus upward and "let go" inside.
The whole spiritual transaction took only a second or two.
In that instant I was acknowledging that this book was
Christ's work not mine and he was free to do with it as he
pleased. Less than a minute later I thought about my fre-
quent habit of temporarily losing things and then this par-

ticular incident with the car keys came flooding back to memory.

Christ in and through Me

When I stopped and prayed about my keys, I was experiencing what some Christian writers have called the "exchanged life."[2] I was consciously exchanging control from my own self to the control of Christ living within me.

As Paul told the Galatians, "I have been crucified with Christ; and it is no longer I who live, but Christ lives in me; and the life which I now live in the flesh I live by faith in the Son of God" (Gal. 2:20). In some ways this picture of faith is similar to the Position in Christ door. In both cases we need to begin by believing that something is true of us. And then by faith we need to move forward in a way that is consistent with what we believe to be true.

In other ways these two doors are opposites. When I use the position door I am picturing myself exalted, sitting at the right hand of the Father. But with the exchanged door, I am picturing myself in the most humble position possible, hanging on a cross, crucified, just as I deserve to be. In the position door, I then begin to act like a royal child of the King. But in the exchanged door, I step out of the way and let Christ rule in my life. Both are transactions of faith, but the biblical pictures are quite distinct.

The Exchanged Life door is an all-or-nothing door. In every moment of every day, either I am in control of my life or Christ is in control. There is no room here for a fifty-fifty (or even a ninety-ten) partnership. Either Christ is given complete control or he's not in control at all! Jesus said, "Apart from Me you can do nothing" (John 15:5). What did he mean? Clearly I can walk, talk, eat, and do many other things without Jesus. After all, total unbelievers do all these things every day for their whole lives.

What Jesus meant was that I can do nothing of eternal significance without him. Whatever I do apart from the control of Christ, no matter how valuable and substantial it looks, will turn out to be merely "wood, hay, straw" (1 Cor. 3:12). It will be burned up in the final judgment. On the other hand, those things that I do when Christ is in control, no matter how common or trivial they seem now, will turn out to be "gold, silver, precious stones" (1 Cor. 3:12).

Dying Yet Living

How does this work? How is it possible for Christ to actually live his life through me? In Romans 6 Paul explains that all genuine Christians have been baptized into Christ's death. The root meaning of the word *baptized* is not "dunked in water" but, rather, "identified." And identification is what Paul has in mind in these verses. When we received Christ, we became identified with (baptized into) his death. Paul goes on to say that we have also been identified with Christ's burial and resurrection. His conclusion and challenge to the Roman Christians and to us is "consider yourselves to be dead to sin, but alive to God in Christ Jesus" (Rom. 6:11). When Paul says we should *consider* ourselves alive in Christ, he means that we should mentally, emotionally, and volitionally count on it as being true. It's as if Paul is saying to us, "Are you dead to sin and alive in Christ? Count on it!" These things are true in God's eyes and we need to grab hold of these truths, cling to them, and begin to live in light of them. So according to the Exchanged Life door, I do play a role in living the Christian life. My role is to get out of the way and allow Christ to live the Christian life in and through me.

"I've tried for twenty years to live the life of a good Christian." Jonathan looked around the ring of faces in his small group in the adult Sunday school class. When no one else spoke, he continued. "I'm a regular churchgoer. I tithe and I've served on my share of committees. I've sung in the choir and taken turns in the nursery."

Everyone was looking at him, wondering what was coming next.

"Actually I'm okay as long as I avoid certain parts of the Bible and don't get stuck listening to a particular sort of sermon."

Since no one else was speaking, I finally said, "What do you mean? Which sections of the Bible? What kinds of sermons?"

Jonathan chuckled wryly. "You know the kind of message, the convicting kind, the sort where the pastor sticks the knife between your ribs and turns it slowly."

"And the Bible verses?" I said.

"Oh, you know—all those black-and-white ones. 'Be perfect as your Father is perfect.' 'Let your righteousness exceed the Pharisees.' 'Sell all you have and give it to the poor.' 'Take up your cross daily and follow me.' There are hundreds of them."

Jonathan let out a long sigh. "I've concluded that the Christian life is just too difficult for any ordinary human being. God expects way too much!"

Jonathan was only partly right. The Christian life is not difficult, it's impossible. God does expect more of us than any fallen human being could ever be. In fact there is only one Man who ever succeeded in living all that God desired—Jesus himself. And he is still the only one who is able to live it. If authentic Christian living is going to happen in Jonathan or in any other Christian, it will be Jesus Christ himself living in and through the believer who accomplishes it.

The Hard Rest

There is a strange paradox in living the Christ-life. Depending on how you look at it, having Christ live through you is either very hard or very easy. Let me explain what I mean.

Here in the West, at the beginning of the twenty-first century, we live in one of the busiest and most complex civilizations the world has ever known. Our lives are crammed with messages from telephone calls, radio, TV, billboards, and computer screens. And we keep inventing new ways to speed up the flow of information—PDAs, cell phones, global positioning devices. And I'm sure the trend will continue. Soon, perhaps before this book is published, I expect you'll be able to buy glasses that will keep you in constant contact with the Internet through pop-up messages programmed to your interests.

For me one of the most difficult things I ever do is simply to be quiet for a few moments. I find it so hard simply to relax and *do nothing.* And yet, in one sense, that is exactly what the exchanged life entails. I must stop my internal frenzy, relax, and allow the life of Christ to flood my consciousness and, in fact, my entire being. So in one way, for me at least, trusting Christ is difficult.

But now here's the paradox. Looked at another way, it is the easiest thing in the world. Because all I have to do is *nothing.* Now I must hasten to admit, it is not exactly what we usually mean when we think of the word *nothing.* Usually a Christ-controlled Christian does not just sit in a room somewhere and meditate eighteen hours a day. The Christ-controlled life is normally filled with activity. But it is activity done from a quiet confidence. After all, it is Christ who is responsible for what I do, where I go, and what I accomplish.

Wait a minute, you may be thinking. *Are you saying that we don't exert any effort when Christ is in control?*

It's a good question. Is the life of a Christ-controlled Christian some kind of blissful euphoria, disconnected from the world around him or her? Clearly the answer must be no.

In the chapter on brokenness, we looked at Paul's description of his own suffering: floggings, stoning, hunger, exhaustion, betrayal, and the intense emotional burden of his ministry. Little wonder that in Romans Paul describes the Christian life by quoting the psalmist, "For Your sake we are being put to death all day long; we were considered as sheep to be slaughtered" (Rom. 8:36, cf. Ps. 44:22). Paul felt the pain and frustration of his life and ministry intensely. And yet he goes on to say, "In all these things we overwhelmingly conquer through Him who loved us" (v. 37). When Christ's love controls us, we are not oblivious to our circumstances, neither do we simply grit our teeth and somehow survive them. Rather, by the power of Christ living in and through us, we rise above even the worst circumstances and "overwhelmingly conquer."

Spiritual Jet Stream

A number of years ago I flew from Los Angeles to Hong Kong to teach a concentrated two-week course. I was amazed to find a direct flight from LAX to Hong Kong Island. While on the flight there, I began examining the printed itinerary I had gotten from my travel agent. I did the math several times and then called the cabin attendant. "I've got a mystery here. I wonder if you could help me solve it."

"I'll try," she said helpfully.

"I've added the flight times, allowing for the difference in time zones and it looks like our flight today will be about fifteen hours. Does that seem right?"

"Yes," she said, "LA to Hong Kong usually takes about fifteen hours."

"And there are no stops, right?"

"That's right. It's a direct flight."

"Well, here's my problem. If I've done the math right, the return flight is only scheduled to be in the air for thirteen hours. How can we get there two hours quicker on the return trip? Do we take a different route or something?"

"No," she said, "the route is nearly identical and the number of miles we travel each direction is about the same. But the mystery is easy to explain. It's the jet stream."

"I've heard of it," I said, "but I don't know exactly what it is."

She smiled. "It's a current of air at a certain elevation that flows one direction for most of the year. On the return trip the plane will actually be flying faster, even though we are using the same amount of fuel."

And sure enough, on the return trip we actually made it to LA in only twelve hours. I guess the jet stream must have been even stronger than usual.

I had a lot of hours to think on those long flights. I realized that the Christ-controlled life is a lot like flying in the jet stream. The pilot doesn't really do anything very different on the return trip than he does on the way to Hong Kong. The primary difference is that he intentionally puts himself (and us) squarely in the path of a powerful force of nature. When it comes to the exchanged life, I choose to place myself into the "path" of the power of Christ living within me. But instead of a natural force, I am now energized by the supernatural power of the eternal Second Person of the Trinity.

Sometimes I am vividly aware of Christ's power and sometimes it is so subtle as to be undetectable. On the way back to LA, I tried to see if I could tell that we were flying at an increased rate. I could not detect any difference at all. The engines sounded the same; the level of vibration felt the same. The only difference I noticed was that the airline showed only two movies instead of the three they showed on the way to Hong Kong. And sometimes it's just the same with the Christ-controlled life. I pray and ask him to take control and I have to believe by faith that he has honored my prayer and is actually living his life through me.

But other times the difference is dramatic. I think one of the reasons I enjoy international ministry so much is that often in other countries I find myself in situations that are way beyond my control. I personally find it easier to trust Christ when it is obvious that I am far outside my own knowledge, resources, or ability to cope.

In 1991 I had the privilege of being a part of the very first International School Project teacher convocation in Moscow. It was held in May, just a few months before the collapse of the Soviet Union. Two hundred Russian school-teachers and administrators attended the first conference. Many of the attendees were high government officials in the Soviet Ministry of Education. I was a part of a team of Western Christians who had been invited to train the teachers to teach Christian ethics and morality in the Russian public school system. My primary role was to introduce the secondary curriculum that I had helped to write and edit during the past several months. There was only one small problem. The curriculum had been translated and printed in Florida and put on a plane for Moscow but had not arrived in time for the conference. It was quite a challenge to stand in front of more than one hundred teachers and try to explain how to use a curriculum they couldn't see.

But that was easy compared to what came next. On the last day of the conference, Blair Cook, my longtime friend and the overall project director, took me aside.

"Alan, as you know, tomorrow the team leaves by train for Volegda, the second conference city. Everybody on the team has a crucial role in the conference except you."

I started to protest, but Blair continued.

"Until we locate the curriculum, you really have noth-ing to introduce. I need you to stay behind here in Moscow and see if you can't find those boxes."

I swallowed hard. "You mean you want me to stay here alone?"

"Yes, but I'll give you money, we've booked a room in this hotel for as long as you need it, and we've engaged an interpreter for as long as you need him. If you find those boxes, bring them with you on the night train and join us in Volegda. If you can't find them in a week, then meet us in Leningrad the week after."

When I woke up the next morning, the whole team had left. It suddenly dawned on me that it was just me and a college-age interpreter—who didn't even know the Lord— against the entire Soviet bureaucracy!

The situation seemed completely impossible. The air-line officials in both the United States and Moscow repeat-edly asserted that the materials could not possibly be in Moscow. One official in New York said, "If we let those packages get on an international flight without the proper paperwork, we'd be violating about a dozen national and international laws. We don't have the paperwork; there-fore, those boxes couldn't have left the U.S.!"[3]

In fact the situation seemed so outrageous, it became easy to turn the whole thing over to Christ. I was obviously grotesquely underqualified. It was my first visit to Russia so I didn't know my way around. I knew only about four words of Russian. I was obviously an American, so Soviet officials at the airport treated me with attitudes that ranged from cool reserve to overt suspicion. All of my graduate degrees were in Bible and theology. I'd never taken even one course in diplomacy or international relations. And my friend Blair had made it painfully clear the exact nature of my primary qualification for the job—I was expendable.

My days were long and tedious as my interpreter and I went from office to office and argued with one uncooperative petty official after another. (I emerged from that week with two convictions: The Soviets invented red tape and Russians under Communism had refined arguing to a high art form!)

But while the activities themselves were banal and wearying, I now look back on that week as one of the most exciting adventures of my life. Why? Because I was trusting Christ for the impossible. Even during those five days in Moscow, I had the overwhelming sense of Christ walking around in my body, directing my path, and guiding my words.

At the end of the fifth day we found the materials in a warehouse at the Moscow airport, where they had been all along. My interpreter put me on the night train and when I arrived the next morning, I was whisked from the station to the conference site where I just had time to introduce the curriculum to the teachers during the very last session!

What was going on that week? I was in the center of God's jet stream, the power of Christ within me. Precisely because I was in so far over my head, it was easy for me to trust Christ to do the impossible. In a strange way the spiritual situation I was facing was not really any different from the one every Christian faces every day of his or her life. It is always true that I can do nothing of spiritual significance without Christ's power within me. The only real difference that week was that it was abundantly apparent to me that the task was hopeless unless I depended on Christ for supernatural wisdom and guidance.

The Challenge of the Everyday

Unfortunately for me, it is not always so obvious that I must depend on Christ for everything. I have learned that my personality type is one that finds it much easier to trust the Lord in extremity and crisis than in the trivial and mundane. I once heard a wonderful story about Ruth Bell Graham, the wife of Billy Graham. Apparently when she had young kids and her life revolved mostly around home-making and child rearing, she had a sign made and hung it over her kitchen sink. It said, "Services of Holy Worship conducted here three times daily." What a wonderful idea—that washing dishes (and I'm sure she had plenty of them in those days) could become an act of worship. I think this intrigues me because it is so foreign to my nat-ural bent. For me, mundane tasks like washing dishes, grading papers, and answering correspondence have always been things I put off as long as I can and then grudg-ingly rush through so I can quickly get on to more stim-ulating and interesting activities. But to see them as an act of worship? Then again, perhaps Ruth Graham had that sign made because she knew she needed to be reminded to view the repetitive aspects of homemaking as acts of worship. All the biographies I've read depict her as an out-going and highly creative person. At least it comforts me to think a woman I so greatly admire may have struggled with the mundane a bit as I do. One of the reasons I often volunteer to pioneer new projects and attempt things that no one has done before is that I often find myself walking more closely with Christ in those situations.

Writings on the Exchanged Life

One of the earliest modern writers to stress this picture of the Christian life was A. B. Simpson (1844–1919), the founder of the Christian and Missionary Alliance. His pre-sentation of the Exchanged Life is in a little book called *The Self Life and the Christ Life*. "The world says, look out for yourself; but Jesus says, 'Not I, but Christ.'"[4] Simpson is very clear that he is talking about a costly commitment subsequent to salvation that not all Christians are ready to experience. "After you receive the baptism of the Holy Ghost, after God comes to live in you, after the Holy Spirit makes your heart His home, then it is that you have to go with Christ into His own dying."[5]

In the second half of the twentieth century the Exchanged Life door has been popularized by Major W. Ian Thomas and other speakers and writers associated with the Torch-bearers (which Thomas founded and directed). The Torchbearers is a deeper-life parachurch organization, which began in England and spread to Canada, the United States, and several other countries. Perhaps the best-known and most influential presentation of the exchanged life was in Thomas's best-selling book *The Saving Life of Christ*. The stress of the book is not on receiving Christ's death as the means of salvation but on the power of Christ's life for day-to-day living.

> If you will but trust Christ, not only for the death He died in order to redeem you, but also for the life that He lives and waits to live through you, the very next step you take will be a step taken in the very energy and power of God Himself. You will have begun to live a life which is essentially supernatural, yet still clothed with the common humanity of your physical body, and still worked out both in the big and the little things that inevitably make up the lot of a man who, though his heart may be with Christ in heaven, still has his two feet firmly planted on the earth.[6]

Near the end of his book, Thomas marks the contrast between the self-life and the Christ-life in the strongest possible terms.

> How much can you do without Him? Nothing! So what is everything you do without Him? Nothing!
>   It is amazing how busy you can be doing nothing! Did you ever find that out? "The flesh"—everything that you

do apart from Him—"profiteth nothing"(John 6:63), and there is always the awful possibility, if you do not discover this principle, that you may spend a lifetime in the service of Jesus Christ *doing nothing!*[7]

Other writers whose books emphasize the same picture of the Christian life include John Hunter and Stuart Briscoe.[8]

This then is the picture of faith we call the Exchanged Life. I cease trying to live the Christian life in my own power and instead, moment by moment, depend on Christ who lives within me and desires to live his life through me. Looked at one way, this is a life of peaceful rest. I can relax, since I am not responsible for the outcome of anything I do. Christ, the eternal God who created me, has taken over the entire responsibility for all that I do. However, looked at in another light, the Exchanged Life is a thrilling adventure as I have a front-row seat to watch the ever surprising deeds of a supernatural God working in my very own life!

Earlier in this chapter, I mentioned Blair Cook, the director of the International School Project. Blair and I have been friends and colleagues for more than twenty-five years. Usually the times I work with Blair begin with a phone call. I hear that warm voice over the phone say, "Hey, Buddy, I got a little project I'd like you to help me with." Sometimes it means flying to some exotic place north of the Arctic Circle.[9] But on other occasions it simply means spending a couple of weeks writing curriculum in a conference center somewhere in the United States or in the International School Project offices in Ohio. Now if you're thinking, *That sounds pretty boring,* you'd be wrong. Partly it's because no time spent around Blair could ever be boring. And partly it's because Blair assembles such incredibly gifted teams to work on these curriculum projects. One exceptional fellow who's been involved in nearly all of them during the last decade is Rex Johnson, a marriage and family counselor and professor at Talbot Seminary. The last time Rex and I roomed together was when Blair pulled together a team to write a set of curricula to accompany the audiocassette "Story of Jesus." God has since used the tape and curriculum packages in an incredible way in nearly all of the sixty-seven thousand schools throughout the entire country of Russia.

I arrived at that particular writing conference first. I knew that Rex had a very rough schedule and had actually left a family vacation early to come and work with us. When I met him at the door of our motel room, I made some comment about being glad he was willing to make the sacrifice to leave his vacation and come to a stuffy office building and write for fourteen to eighteen hours a day. It was then Rex said something I'll never forget. What he said expressed, better than I ever could, exactly the way I feel. And it also summarizes quite well the adventure of living the Exchanged Life.

Rex said, "I like to respond to Blair because when he calls, it's always with a God-sized task."

SEVEN

DOOR 5
BECOME
A TRUE
DISCIPLE
Disciplined Life

I need to begin this chapter with a confession. The discipline door into faith is definitely not my door! I think I need to tell you this right up front because you're going to figure it out sooner or later anyway. As in my chapters on each of the other doors, I'm going to include stories from my own life to illustrate this picture of faith. But if you've progressed very far in any of the spiritual disciplines yourself, or even if you've read any of the standard books on the subject, you're going to quickly see how pitiful and anemic my personal illustrations really are, so I decided I'd better be candid with you from the beginning.

You may be wondering why I am including this door into faith in my book. There are several reasons. First, and most important, the Bible has quite a lot to say about this door of faith. Second, it is a door on which influential past and present Christian leaders have spoken and written extensively. Third, this door has helped many believers toward a more consistent walk of faith. Therefore I felt it was quite important to include it.

There is also a more personal reason why I felt it essential to examine this door. As I said earlier, often the doors that come least naturally or intuitively to us are the ones we most need in order to grow on toward maturity in Christ. Personally I have found the steps I have taken through this door (infrequent and tentative though they may have been) have yielded great benefit. So if you already know you are like me, and may be tempted to skip this door entirely, read on. This just might be the most important chapter in the book for your future growth in faith.

Maturity and Fruit

"I don't get it," I said. "Why do more mature Christians often see greater fruit in their Christian lives than brand-new believers?"

I was sitting across from Swede Anderson, the national campus ministry director for Campus Crusade for Christ. I was a first-year staff member and still a fairly new believer. I had asked for the meeting to answer some theological questions that had been bothering me.

Swede listened thoughtfully. "Why should it surprise you that a seasoned believer is more fruitful than a baby one?"

"Well," I said, "new believers have the same Holy Spirit, don't they? All of Christ comes to live inside them the moment they are born spiritually."

"Yes, that's true."

"And it's God who brings people to himself, not our wisdom or convincing arguments, isn't it?"

"Also quite true." There was just a hint of a smile in the corners of Swede's eyes—I think he'd figured out where I was going.

"So it seems to me," I continued, "that a new believer should be just as effective in evangelism as a more experienced one. Why doesn't it work out that way?"

"It's a good question," Swede said. "Let me try to explain with a couple of analogies. Suppose you have a huge volume of water rushing downhill. Let's say a hundred thousand gallons per minute."

"Okay," I said.

"And let's imagine that water is all in a narrow, deep, steep gorge. What would that be like?"

"Uhh . . . a lot of power—a lot of force."

"That's right. It could uproot any trees in its way and move huge boulders. And if we built a dam and a power generator across that gorge, we could light a small city. That would be focused, usable power."

"Yes, I understand," I said.

"Now, let's imagine the same volume of water—a hundred thousand gallons a minute—but instead of a gorge, we turn it loose on a wide, flat plain, many miles across. How would that be different?"

"Well," I said, "the water would flow much more slowly and it wouldn't be as deep."

"That's right. The force would be dissipated over a wide area. And now the water would simply flow slowly around things like rocks and trees. You'd have a little water everywhere, but none of it would have a very great effect. In fact most of it would probably sink into the ground."

"So the Holy Spirit is like the water in your analogy, is that right?"

"Exactly," said Swede. "A new believer has the same power of the Holy Spirit as a mature one. But in a mature believer that power is channeled and focused, like the water rushing down the gorge."

"I guess that makes sense," I said.

"Or how about this analogy? Have you ever used a shotgun?"

"Not really," I said, "but I have a pretty good idea what they do."

"Well, then, you know that a shotgun shoots a large number of small pellets, or shot, that quickly spread out over a wide area. Especially if you are aiming some distance away, you can do a little bit of damage over a large region." Swede chuckled. "They're great for people like me who don't have very good aim!"

I smiled at the mental picture of Swede blasting away blindly and made a mental note not to go on any hunting trips with him!

"Now compare that with an M-1 rifle. In the hands of a sharpshooter, it can concentrate a lot of force behind a single bullet at a much greater distance than a shotgun.

"New believers are kind of like the shotgun—they splatter a little bit of God's power all over the place."

I smiled, remembering some of my early attempts at sharing my faith.

"But a mature, trained, and experienced believer is much more like the powerful rifle. He or she can concentrate God's power on the very spot where it is needed."

"I think I understand," I said. "But how, exactly, does a person become a deep, powerful channel for the Holy Spirit?"

Swede smiled. "Some of it is just walking with the Lord over many years. But some of that channeling comes from the spiritual disciplines."

"Which disciplines do you mean, in particular?"

"Well, all of them really—prayer, Bible study and meditation, fasting. Even witnessing itself is a discipline. And they not only help us to be a more effective witness, but the disciplines can benefit every area of our Christian lives. They can give us a closer relationship with God, help us understand and teach his Word more effectively, and give us a more consistent victory over sin. In short, the disciplines can help us mature in our walk of faith."

Free from Fear

What exactly do we mean by Christian discipline or the disciplines of the Christian life? If you look in a standard English dictionary, you will find two primary meanings for the word (at least in its basic verb form). The first is "to train" or "to bring to a condition of order or obedience, bring under control." As we'll see in a minute, this is very close to some of the biblical uses of "discipline." But it's the second common English definition that gets us into trouble. The second definition is "to punish, chastise." Isn't that often what we think of when we hear the word *discipline?* The New Testament teaching about Christian discipline is always in the first sense of training or teaching. Let me say this as clearly as I can: The New Testament *never* speaks of God punishing believers.

As I see it, this is one of the primary differences between the Old Covenant that God gave Israel at Sinai and the New Covenant we enjoy as Christians. In the Old Covenant God basically said to the Jews, "Obey me and I'll reward you, disobey and I'll punish you." But the New Covenant is very different—it is motivated by love and understanding. It is clear, even in the Old Testament, that God's highest desire was not for believers to respond to him out of fear. Speaking through the prophet Ezekiel about the coming New Covenant, the Lord says, "I will give you a new heart with new and right desires, and I will put a new spirit in you. I will take out your stony heart of sin and give you a new, obedient heart" (Ezek. 36:26 NLT). And in the New Testament Paul echoes the prophet's words when he declares that the Christians in Rome "became obedient from the heart" (Rom. 6:17). While the Old Covenant was motivated by fear, God now wants us to respond to him out of love, and the two are ultimately incompatible. John, who is often called "the disciple of love," explains it this way. "There is no fear in love. But perfect love drives out fear, because fear has to do with punishment. The one who fears is not made perfect in love" (1 John 4:18 NIV). God knew all along that he would never have a genuine love relationship with us as long as we were afraid he was going to punish us. Therefore he put the punishment for our sin on Christ and now offers us a love relationship free from fear.

Our New Covenant relationship with God is not only motivated by love but it comes with understanding. Jesus told his followers, "I no longer call you servants, because a servant does not know his master's business. Instead, I have called you friends, for everything that I learned from my Father I have made known to you" (John 15:15 NIV). David, the man after God's own heart (1 Sam. 13:14; Acts 13:22), elaborates the same idea: "The LORD says, 'I will guide you along the best pathway for your life. I will advise you and watch over you. Do not be like a senseless horse or mule that needs a bit and bridle to keep it under control'" (Ps. 32:8–9 NLT).

What is David saying about the Lord's attitude toward us? He's saying God does not want a relationship based on the fear of punishment. Do you know how a bit and bridle work? A bit is a piece of metal placed inside an animal's mouth. It's put there because the mouth is very tender and sensitive to pain. The bit attaches to the bridle. The rider holds reins, which also attach to the bridle. When the rider pulls on the reins, the bit causes pain in the animal's mouth. So the animal turns its head to relieve the pressure and thereby lessen the pain. And where the animal's head goes, the rest of the body inevitably follows. The rider can then turn the animal to the left or the right with no resistance. It's a system based entirely on the threat and avoidance of pain.

But let's imagine for a moment that a farmer wants to try a different system—one based on understanding. The farmer goes out to his barn and stands in front of his mule.

"Mule," says the farmer, "it's springtime and we need to go out to the field and plow it up to plant our grain. And I want you to understand, this is not only for me. In that field we're also going to raise the grain for your feed. Next winter when it's cold and there's no grass to graze on, you'll be really glad we plowed this field today and raised some grain for you to eat. Now that you can see it's in your own enlightened self-interest to plow that field, let's get started!"

And the farmer waits while the mule stares at him with a blank expression. What's wrong? Like the Lord says, the mule has no sense, no understanding. If the farmer really wants his field plowed, he'll have to get out the bit and bridle. But God says he doesn't want us to be like the mule. Rather he wants a relationship where he guides and advises us. He wants a relationship where we follow him because we understand what he is doing and know that his plan is best for us.

This is why Christian discipline is never used in the New Testament in the sense of punishment. God does not need to punish us for our sins; all of our punishment fell on Christ. When we believe we have nothing to fear from God, then we are ready to willingly enter into godly discipline based on love and understanding.

Further Defining Discipline

With that understanding of discipline in mind, let me give you my own definition of Christian discipline. *Discipline is the willing yielding of an immediate pleasure or whim to reach a more important long-range goal.* I'd like to take a moment to look at several words in that definition and explain what I mean by them. When I say that discipline is the *willing* yielding of immediate pleasure, I mean that our choice must be made freely. Discipline will not work, long-term, if it is entered into under coercion or a fear of punishment.

By "immediate pleasure or whim" I mean the passing things we all desire. We all want good things to eat, a comfortable place to live, rest and relaxation, enjoyable hobbies and entertainment, and the respect and admiration of others. Oh yes, and money, lots of money. Now none of these things is bad in itself.[1] In fact Jesus promised that God would provide his followers with all they truly need (Matt. 6:25–34). The problem comes when the desire for any of these things gets in the way of growing in our relationship with God. It seems that these things often do, especially here in the wealthy West. Godly discipline says, "I choose to set aside my temporary fun or comfort or security, so I can draw closer to God and seek his best for me."

And, finally, what do I mean by "a more important long-range goal"? Ultimately all of God's plans for us are long-range plans. He created us with eternity in mind. He designed us to know and love him forever. He made us to be like him and reflect his image. He knows that we will not ultimately be happy or fulfilled unless we are growing toward maturity in him. So he continually invites us to set aside the temporary, immediate pleasures to work toward a long-term joy that is beyond measure.

That is what I think the New Testament means when it talks about discipline. Discipline is the willing yielding of an immediate pleasure or whim to reach a more important long-range goal.

"Do you have to leave right away? We haven't been here very long. I hate to eat and run." Jan looked at me from the other end of the couch with those lovely dark eyes of hers. In more than thirty years of marriage, I've never found it easy to say no to her—and so I rarely do!

"Sure, we can stay another half hour or so."

After a long day, we'd gratefully accepted an invitation to have dinner with Jan's mom, who lives near us in our small mountain town. And I really was enjoying myself. We were all watching a fascinating breaking news story on CNN.[2] I'm a bit of a news junkie and could have happily stayed and watched for another hour or two. Besides, I knew that soon Jan's mom would offer me dessert. (There are always several yummy options lurking in her fridge.)

Then Jan said, "If you need to write this evening, I'll drive you home now and then come back and spend some more time with Mom."

My mind darted back over the last two months. It had been that long since I'd done the last serious work on this book. First, an unexpected writing opportunity had come up. Then I'd been so sick for two weeks that I'd gotten little done on the book. I'd recovered just in time to make a scheduled teaching trip to Russia from which I'd returned unusually badly jet-lagged. That was just a week ago. Now the clock was ticking. Only twenty days left until the completed manuscript had to be sent to Baker!

I had a choice to make—a warm relaxing home, good company, CNN, and dessert or a date with a cold downstairs office and a blinking computer cursor.

"Thanks, honey," I said. "I think you'd better drop me at home."

Why did I choose to go home? On this occasion (for a change) I chose the route of discipline. I willingly yielded the immediate pleasure of CNN and dessert for the more important long-range goal of completing the manuscript on time and doing the best possible job on this book.

Our Incredible Example

Buried deep in the Book of Hebrews is the most compelling example of godly discipline. It is the example of Jesus himself. The twelfth chapter begins by encouraging us to run the race of the Christian life with endurance. "Let us also lay aside every encumbrance and the sin which so easily entangles us, and let us run with endurance the race that is set before us" (Heb. 12:1). Then the writer points us to Jesus as our example of godly discipline. "Fixing our eyes on Jesus, the author and perfecter of faith, who for the joy set before Him endured the cross" (Heb. 12:2). What an incredible verse! I think I could write a whole chapter, maybe even a whole book, just on this one verse. But instead, I'll content myself with a few brief observations.

First, like a runner who mentally blocks out everything and everyone else and simply concentrates on the finish line, we are to live our lives focused on Jesus. He himself is our finish line. But he is not just the goal we are striving toward, he is also the one who got us into the race; he is the author of our faith. And beyond that, he is also the perfecter of our faith. He is the one living inside us who provides the power and endurance to finish the race. But now comes the best part. He is the ultimate example of discipline. The verse says he endured the cross "for the joy set before Him." What was that joy? What was the long-range goal that allowed Jesus to set aside his own desires and willingly accept the agony of the cross?

When I first read this verse, I thought that the "joy set before Him" might have been restored fellowship with the

Father. But later I realized that Jesus did not need to go to the cross to achieve that. Unbroken fellowship with the Father had been his from all eternity. And then it hit me. What was the one thing Jesus could not have unless he endured the cross? It was fellowship with us fallen humans. When Jesus went to the cross, he was thinking of you and of me. The joy that drew Jesus, the greater long-range goal that motivated him to accept the pain of the cross, was the anticipation of a love relationship with you and me. Even as I am writing these words, there are tears welling in my eyes. It is unbelievable that Jesus could want a relationship with us so much that he would accept the entire righteous anger of a holy God against sin and willingly endure separation from the Father he knew so intimately and loved so deeply.

Our Encouraging Promise

Later in this same chapter of Hebrews, there is a crucial bit of encouragement I badly need every time I think about any type of discipline. The writer promises us that any regimen of discipline gets easier as we go along. "All discipline for the moment seems not to be joyful, but sorrowful; yet to those who have been trained by it, afterwards it yields the peaceful fruit of righteousness" (Heb. 12:11). What does this mean? It is saying that all discipline is the most difficult and painful in the beginning. But as we go along, it begins to get easier until, finally, we are fully trained and it has become easiest and most natural to do what is right. That is what the phrase "the peaceful fruit of righteousness" means. It is talking about the time when our habitual patterns have been so thoroughly reshaped that doing what is right is no longer hard at all but has become our instinctive and natural way of life.

Habits, Addiction, and Freedom

I want to say a bit about the relationship between discipline and addiction. They are the flip sides of something fundamental God has built into our nature as human beings. God created us to be habitual creatures. We are not simply creatures of instinct; rather, we humans have an incredible capacity to learn and grow. This is true in the physical, mental, emotional, and spiritual realms. If you have ever practiced an athletic skill or developed a musical talent, you know exactly what I mean. All of these require practice, practice, and more practice.

I was never much of an athlete, but I began college as a music major and at one time or another took lessons in singing, guitar, piano, and string bass. Whenever I'd begin a new instrument or even a distinctly different skill on the same one, I'd have the same experience. I'd feel like a klutz. It would seem like I was never going to do anything but make ugly noises. But after hours and hours of scales, after days and weeks of forcing my fingers to do the same boring thing again and again, something wonderful would gradually begin. More and more often my fingers would go where they were supposed to go. And like an opening flower, the sounds I was making gradually transformed from ordinary to beautiful. And something else began to happen. I began to feel liberated. Once I had mastered the basics, I could begin to improvise. Once I'd learned the scales and chords so well that they were second nature, I was freed to experiment and create my own music.

So far I've been talking about constructive kinds of habits. But there is another kind, the kind we call addiction. An addiction does not liberate; it imprisons. A constructive habit gives you greater control over your mind and body. An addiction gives you less control—it begins to control you. Why do addictions exist? They are simply another example of our fall into sin, taking something God created for our good and warping it into something that hurts us. C. S. Lewis believed that everything evil, every temptation, was simply something good God had made that had been bent or warped away from its intended purpose.[3] I think Lewis was right. This is a helpful way to think about the connection between discipline and addiction. God has made us in such a way that we will become habituated to something. If we do not learn to eat healthy food, we'll eat fast food or junk food and we'll naturally become habituated to them and want more of them. If we don't develop a habit of exercise, we'll become habituated to our couch-potato lifestyle and it will be even harder to exercise in the future.

Humans can become habituated to almost anything, even unpleasant things. I never drank coffee until I was a freshman in college. The few times I tried it, I thought it was a bitter, unpleasant drink. Then for one semester, I had a very early, boring class where I sat in the back and often fell asleep. A few weeks into the term I realized I'd better find a way to stay awake or I was going to flunk. So every morning I'd blow through the student center and grab their biggest, strongest cup of coffee. By the end of the semester I was hooked! By then I'd decided it wasn't such a foul drink after all. In fact I'd actually begun to enjoy the taste.

This is the same process by which people become habituated (addicted) to cigarettes and cigars, extreme violence in movies, abusive relationships, and many other ugly things. The human personality is surprisingly elastic. Things that start out unpleasant or even revolting, if we repeat them often enough, soon become commonplace, then expected, then needed.

So the discipline of the spiritual life is just taking this universal principle of how God made us and putting it to the use he intended. I'm convinced he made us habitual creatures, at least partly, so that we could repeatedly choose to seek him. As we do, we gradually develop an increasing habituation (dependence) on him. But this is the ultimate example of a habit that is freeing. It is only as we become fully dependent on him that we find our ultimate liberation. As Jesus said, "Whoever loses his life for My sake will find it" (Matt. 16:25) and "If the Son makes you free, you will be free indeed" (John 8:36). This is a part of the great paradox of kingdom life. The way up is down, you must lose to find, dependence brings freedom, and true peace comes only through struggle.

Let me illustrate this idea of the peaceful fruit of righteousness coming through discipline by one final mundane personal example. When Jan and I were first married, we lived in a small upstairs apartment. We both worked the same hours and usually carpooled. The following sequence of events occurred many times in the early months of our marriage.

I would walk in and immediately drop my keys and sunglasses by the front door. Then I'd go to the kitchen, leaving my notebook, books, and papers on the pass-through. On the way to the bedroom, I'd deposit my jacket over the back of a chair or toss it on the couch. As I entered the bedroom, off would come my shirt, which I'd toss in the direction of the doorknob. Sometimes I'd make it; sometimes it would slump to the floor where it would stay. On the way to the bed, I'd kick off my shoes, which would come to rest somewhere between the door and the nightstand.

Before I go any further with my story, you need to understand that Jan and I were raised in very different kinds of homes. When we were dating, Jan's home seemed to me like something out of a fifties sitcom. You could visit, unannounced, any time day or night and the place would be immaculate. And more important to me as a single guy, the cupboards and refrigerator were always crammed with good things to eat. I never remember having a meal there without at least two kinds of homemade dessert. And the leftovers! It was a scrounger's heaven.

And I was not the only one who was impressed. One time the *San Jose Mercury News* actually sent a photographer over to take a picture of Jan's mom in her kitchen. It appeared the next Sunday on the front page of the "living" section with an article naming Jan's mom "homemaker of the month." I'm not kidding. I saw the picture. I read the article.

My home was another story. My mom loved to garden and so our yard was always a showplace. But she was a lot less interested in housekeeping. Some might describe the house I grew up in as "comfortable." Others might call it "casual." But most would say it was just plain messy! Frequently cobwebs lined the ceiling. In our family we'd let the dishes pile up in the kitchen until there weren't enough left in the cupboards to set the table. Then we'd wash some. If company was coming, we'd all go into a high state of frenzy and get everything clean and neat, usually finishing just as the doorbell rang. And as for food, about the best thing I ever found rummaging through our kitchen was Pop-Tarts or packets of Carnation Instant Breakfast.

So in our early months of marriage, Jan and I were both experiencing a bit of culture shock. I'm sure it was much harder for Jan to adjust than for me. But I did become aware of how nice it was to have an apartment that was always neat and clean. And then I began to notice that there was this person following me around picking up the things I'd just dropped. Why, imagine that! It was my lovely bride, Jan! That was when the Holy Spirit began to gently nudge my conscience. Jan was working about as many hours as I was outside the home. And she was making most of the meals and keeping the place clean and neat. It just didn't seem fair that she should have to pick up after me as well.

"Okay, Lord," I said. "From now on I'm going to start putting away my own belongings and hanging up my own clothes."

At first it was like Chinese water torture. I'd get all the way to the bedroom and remember that I'd dropped my keys by the door. Or I'd reach the closet and have to go back to the living room and retrieve my jacket. It seemed like I was spending all my time going back for things. But after a couple of weeks of trying, I found that some of the time I remembered and got all the way to the bedroom without dropping anything. Then pretty soon I was remembering about half the time. That's when I began to be encouraged that I was really making progress. Pretty soon it was the exception when I dropped something. After several months, the new habit was pretty firmly in place. I'd actually feel funny if I happened to leave something out. It was becoming second nature to pick up after myself. And I made a strange discovery. It didn't really feel like it was taking any extra time at all. It was now so habitual that I didn't even have to think about it. I had reached the stage of the "peaceful fruit of righteousness" with regard to picking up after myself. It was now easier to do what was right.

I guess the example of picking up my clothes is a rather minor one. My habits in that area could be substantially changed in a few months. But I believe the same principle applies to any of the godly disciplines. When we first try to have a quiet time, when we first set up a regular time for prayer, when we first attempt to witness—it seems very hard, like we'll never get the hang of it. But each time we practice the discipline, the new, godly habit becomes stronger. And I believe it is an achievable goal in each of our lifetimes to reach the point in any of these disciplines where we experience "the peaceful fruit of righteousness." We eventually find it is easier to do what is right. A day without Bible study and prayer seems strange and empty.

It is the exception when we pass up an opportunity to share our faith. We actually look forward to extended times of prayer and fasting.

I wish I could tell you that I have reached the "peaceful fruit of righteousness" in each of these disciplines. But I can't. I'm further along in some of them than in others. But I'm painfully aware that I'm not as far down the trail in any of them as I should be for the number of years I have walked with the Lord. So I think I'll change the subject slightly and talk about a topic on which I'm something of an expert: things that get in the way of discipline.

Barriers to Discipline

One of the greatest barriers to spiritual discipline for those of us in Western culture is simply the society around us. We live in a society where most of our focus is on externals—how people look, how much they earn, the size of their house, the make of their car, what they've accomplished. As many authors have noted, we are often human *doings,* rather than human *beings.* We know very little about how to stop all our activity and simply be. This presents a real barrier to many of the spiritual disciplines. So many of them must be pursued alone and in a place that is quiet. Many Americans never experience total quiet any time during the day. The clock radio or timer on the TV wakes them up in the morning to music or news. The radio or TV is on while they make and eat breakfast. They jump in the car, on goes the radio or the CD player. Work is filled with conversation (often with a radio talk show bleating away in the background). Dinner and the evening are accompanied by the television. Little wonder that prayer and meditation feel so foreign, like something a Martian might do.

Sometimes your basic personality can form a barrier. If you are a hard-charging type A person, or if you are very goal-oriented and have a high need for closure, the disciplines are counterintuitive, because it's so hard to "keep score." Sure you can mark off three more chapters on your read-through-the-Bible-in-a-year sheet. But most of our true progress in the disciplines has to do with how they change us within. Are we closer to God? Is our faith growing stronger? These are difficult to measure and impossible to precisely quantify.

I have found my own personality to be a barrier. I'm an adventurer and an innovator. I crave excitement, novelty, and experimentation. These traits come in handy when developing new approaches to teaching or doing missionary work in the former Soviet Union, but for the disciplines to be really effective, any of them must be approached with regularity and consistency. It is possible to write a short article or cram for an exam in a day or two. (I know—I've done both.) But true progress toward holiness does not happen in a day or a week or even a month. Becoming more holy can be accomplished only over the course of many years.

What is the solution to these barriers? First, I think we must drink deeply of the patience of our heavenly Father. When I begin (yet another) plan for personal devotions or Bible study and find a few weeks or months into it that I've missed three days in a row, I get frustrated and then discouraged. But God is not frustrated with me nor is he discouraged. Rather he waits patiently for me, urging me forward, cheering me on.

The second answer is the one we've already examined in Hebrews. We need to concentrate on Jesus. He is both our best example of discipline and the internal power and motivation to continue. And, finally, like a runner who has slipped and fallen, we need to get back up again and get back in the race.

A Discipline Door?

In this chapter on discipline, I've taken rather a different approach than most of the books on the subject. Most books on discipline focus on specific individual disciplines (prayer, fasting, Scripture memory, and others). I've concentrated on the broader issues of trying to explain exactly what godly discipline is and is not and looking at things that might motivate us to pursue the various disciplines. I've concentrated on motivation rather than "how-tos" partly because I constantly need all the motivation I can get! But I also sense that many Christians, especially in the West, struggle to keep motivated to continue (or restart) the spiritual disciplines.

Classic exponents of the Christian disciplines include Andrew Murray in *The School of Obedience* and Elisabeth Elliot in *Discipline: The Glad Surrender.* Current writers who emphasize this door into faith include Jerry Bridges in *The Practice of Godliness,* Richard Ganz in *The Secret of Self-Control,* Dallas Willard in *The Spirit of the Disciplines,* and Richard Foster in *Celebration of Discipline: The Path to Spiritual Growth.*

There is one final question I feel I must try to answer before I end this chapter. Some may wonder if spiritual disciplines are a door into faith at all. I believe they are. Clearly, the current authors who are writing widely read books on the subject believe that the disciplines are a path that leads to spiritual power. Let me briefly quote two examples. Richard Foster expresses it this way:

> When we despair of gaining inner transformation through human powers of will and determination, we are open to a wonderful new realization: inner righteousness is a gift from God to be graciously received. . . .
>
> The moment we grasp this breathtaking insight we are in danger of an error in the opposite direction. We are tempted to believe there is nothing we can do. . . .

Happily there is something we can do. God has given us the Disciplines of the spiritual life as a means of receiving his grace. The Disciplines allow us to place ourselves before God so that he can transform us.[4]

Dallas Willard expresses a similar idea in quite different words:

Today, we think of Christ's power entering our lives in various ways—through the sense of forgiveness and love for God or through the awareness of truth, through special experiences or the infusion of the Spirit, through the presence of Christ in the inner life.[5]

The Spirit of the Disciplines is nothing but the love of Jesus with its resolute will to be like him whom we love. In the fellowship of the burning heart, "exercise unto godliness" is our way of receiving ever more fully the grace in which we stand.[6]

There is no question in my mind that for many, including these two authors, the disciplines are doors into a deeper, maturing, consistent walk with Christ. The various spiritual disciplines, when entered willingly, can become crucial stepping-stones toward a richer and more consistent life of faith.

EIGHT

DOOR 6
WALK IN
THE SPIRIT
Spirit Filled

Witnessing is fine for you, Alan." My roommate, Nick, sat upright at his tiny desk. I was slouched on my bed against the opposite wall of our dorm room, a few feet away.

"You've got an outgoing personality," Nick continued. "It's all so new and exciting for you. But I'm the quieter, more studious type."

Much of what Nick was saying rang true. We made odd roommates—a real study in contrasts. Nick was neat and meticulous; I was a bit of a slob. He was very disciplined about his homework and spent hours studying each day. I was much more casual and liked to socialize. He had gotten straight *A*s all through high school and junior college. I had a *C* average in high school and felt lucky to be getting *B*s in most of my college classes. I was tall, gregarious, and dated as often as I could, usually twice a week or more. Nick was short, introverted, and had never been out with a girl, that I was aware of. Nick had been raised in a conservative Christian home and faithfully attended church several times a week all his years growing up. I had received Christ as a college sophomore, less than a year before, and still had lots of questions about my newfound faith.

But something bothered me about what Nick was saying.

"Do you mean God wants me to share my faith but not you?"

"I'm not exactly saying that." Nick looked uncomfortable. "I just think that you'd be a lot more effective than I would. It's not just personality. You can identify with nonbelievers—tell them what it was like before you received Christ. I don't really have a testimony, since I grew up with it."

I wasn't sure how to respond to that, so I was quiet for a moment. Then a thought hit me.

"What about the filling of the Spirit?"

"You mean speaking in tongues?" Nick wrinkled his nose. "My church doesn't hold with that kind of thing."

"No, I just mean being filled with the Spirit by faith."

"I'm not sure what you're talking about."

I was astonished. I had learned how to be filled and empowered by the Holy Spirit at a Campus Crusade for Christ college conference a month after I'd received Christ. I just assumed all Christians understood the concept, especially ones who'd grown up in the church like Nick.

I reached over and dug around in the back of my desk drawer.

"Here," I said, handing over a small booklet. "You've seen one of these before, haven't you?"

"Not sure I have," said Nick. And then he read the cover out loud. "'Have you made the wonderful discovery of the Spirit-filled life?' It looks kind of like a 'Four Spiritual Laws' booklet, except it's blue. Is it another gospel tract?"

"No," I said. "It's written for Christians to help them experience God's power by being filled with the Holy Spirit." I shook my head. "I still can't believe there's something to do with Christianity that I know about and you don't."

Nick grinned modestly. "You'd be surprised what I don't know."

I felt a little awkward. "Uhh . . . I guess we could read through it together and talk about it, if you want to."

"I'd like that," he said.

The little blue booklet that Nick and I discussed that day in our dorm room presents the last of our six doors into faith, the Spirit Filled door. During the past fifty years this picture of the Christian life has been spread throughout the United States and many other countries by Bill Bright and the staff of Campus Crusade for Christ. But Dr. Bright did not invent this "door." This approach to Christian living has been widely disseminated by the Keswick movement since the late 1800s. And, of course, it is found in the pages of the Bible.

Three Kinds of People

In writing to the rebellious and worldly church at Corinth, Paul describes three kinds of people. At any point in time, every person on the face of the earth exists in one of three relationships with the Holy Spirit (whether he or she is aware of it or not).

Those without the Spirit

Paul first talks about nonbelievers, those who do not have God's Spirit in them at all. "The man without the Spirit does not accept the things that come from the Spirit of God, for they are foolishness to him, and he cannot understand them, because they are spiritually discerned" (1 Cor. 2:14 NIV). Paul says that non-Christians are not able to grasp spiritual truth. It seems foolish to them.

Spirit-Filled Christians

The second group of people Paul mentions are those who are filled (controlled and empowered) by the Holy Spirit. "The spiritual man makes judgments about all things, but he himself is not subject to any man's judgment: 'For who has known the mind of the Lord that he may instruct him?' But we have the mind of Christ" (vv. 15–16 NIV). Unlike those without the Spirit, spiritual Christians can accurately discern the truth of God. They actually have access to the mind of Christ himself!

Worldly (Self-Filled) Christians

Finally, Paul centers in on the problem of the Corinthian Christians and identifies the third group of people, worldly Christians. "Brothers, I could not address you as spiritual but as worldly—mere infants in Christ. I gave you milk, not solid food, for you were not yet ready for it. Indeed, you are still not ready" (3:1–2 NIV). Paul goes on to say that these worldly Corinthian Christians were characterized by jealousy, quarreling, sexual immorality, drunkenness, and pride. Instead of trying to build up other Christians, each one was trying to show his or her own importance.

After we receive Christ, once the Holy Spirit has entered us at the moment of spiritual birth, we have the choice to live as spiritual or as worldly Christians. This is not primarily a matter of outward behavior (although our spirituality or worldliness does tend to affect our actions). It is primarily a matter of inward attitude.

Being filled with the Spirit brings the fullness of all that God intended life to be (John 10:10). It is a life filled with love, joy, and power. As Paul promised the Galatians, "When the Holy Spirit controls our lives, he will produce this kind of fruit in us: love, joy, peace, patience, kindness, goodness, faithfulness, gentleness, and self-control" (Gal. 5:22–23 NLT). I don't know any Christians who don't, at their best moments, long to be like this. (And I also don't know any who don't, even at their worst moments, wish they were married to someone like this!) In his last earthly statement to his disciples, Jesus promised that the Holy Spirit would bring us the power to share the gospel with the world. "But you will receive power when the Holy Spirit comes on you; and you will be my witnesses in Jerusalem, and in all Judea and Samaria, and to the ends of the earth" (Acts 1:8 NIV).

Paul also warned the Galatian Christians about the dangers of living without the filling of the Spirit:

> When you follow the desires of your sinful nature, your lives will produce these evil results: sexual immorality, impure thoughts, eagerness for lustful pleasure, idolatry, participation in demonic activities, hostility, quarreling, jealousy, outbursts of anger, selfish ambition, divisions, the feeling that everyone is wrong except those in your own little group, envy, drunkenness, wild parties, and other kinds of sin.
>
> Galatians 5:19–21 NLT

I want to stop for a moment and clarify something. As you read Paul's words, you may be thinking, *I certainly don't keep idols around the house or get involved with demons. I don't drink or go to wild parties. But I do struggle with impure thoughts. I do sometimes get jealous or angry. So does that mean I'm a worldly Christian or a spiritual one?*

The answer is that Paul is talking about overall life tendencies. Both lifestyles are cumulative. The longer a Christian is Spirit-filled, the more the fruit of the Spirit will be
evident in his or her life. The opposite is also true. When
Christians allow their sinful or worldly nature to domi-
nate their lives, the kinds of problems Paul lists tend to
grow worse. And often we fight the battle against our
fleshly nature internally, in our thought lives. Particularly
if we are attending church or living around other Christians, we may sin in our minds but restrain our behavior
for fear of what others would think of us. We may enter-
tain private sexual fantasies but not act on them. We may
feel hostile or angry but keep it inside. We may feel highly
critical of other believers but are careful not to express our
criticism too strongly. Both faith and worldliness are primarily attitudes of the heart. Only over time do they both
tend to become evident in our outward behavior.

A Clean House

Are there any prerequisites to being filled with the
Spirit? Are there things that will prevent us from being
filled? The answer to both questions is yes. The primary
hindrance to being filled is double-mindedness (James
1:6–8). Over the years I've met many Christians who feel
ambivalent toward walking with God. "I'd like to be filled
with the Spirit but there're just one or two things I don't
want God to change." These believers want to put one foot
in the life of the Spirit and keep one foot in the world.
They want to hang on to one or two pet sins but give the
rest of their lives to God. It doesn't work that way. The
Lord of heaven and earth wants to be Lord of your life.
You have a choice. You can be the lord of your own life,
or you can allow him to be your Lord. What you can't do

is set up a partnership. "Okay, Lord, you take 80 percent and I'll just keep this 20 percent for myself."

I'm not saying that we have to somehow clean up our own lives before we can be filled with the Spirit. In fact it is impossible for us to clean house. Especially when an adult Christian has allowed a particular sin to become habitual over many years, it may be utterly impossible to stop that particular sin, even for a day or two. What I am saying is that we have to be willing for God to change us.

How then do we get our house clean enough for the Holy Spirit to fill us? There is only one way—by the blood of Christ. Becoming clean is a supernatural work of God. What we must do is confess that we are sinful and accept his forgiveness. The rest is up to him. "If we confess our sins, He is faithful and righteous to forgive us our sins and to cleanse us from all unrighteousness" (1 John 1:9).

So what are the prerequisites to being filled? We must choose to give everything we are over into his hands. We cannot consciously hold anything back. Then we must accept Christ's forgiveness for all our sins. Now we are ready to be filled.

Command and Promise

How can you or I or any Christian actually be filled with the Holy Spirit? Practically speaking, how can we begin moving toward that life of love and joy and power the Bible promises? Many Christians wrongly believe that being spiritual is something only reserved for ministers or great saints, or it's something that comes only after years of struggle. But God has actually made it very simple for us to be filled with the Spirit. Once we've met the prerequisites, all we need to do is accept his command and trust his promise.

His Command

In his letter to the Ephesians, Paul gives all Christians both a warning and a command. "Do not get drunk with wine, for that is dissipation, but be filled with the Spirit" (Eph. 5:18). This verse contains a fascinating contrast. We should not get drunk, because when we get drunk, we give the control of our mind, emotions, and body over to a foreign substance, alcohol. But then Paul commands us to be "filled with the Spirit." Why does he mention both things in the same verse? Because there is a connection. When we are filled with the Spirit we are giving up control of ourselves—not to a substance like alcohol but to a Person, God the Holy Spirit. Just as a person wrongly gives up control of himself or herself to wine, we are to rightly give up control of ourselves to the Holy Spirit. It's important to notice that being filled is a command. It is something God intends for every Christian. It is not optional. It's not for some specially called or gifted Christians. It is God's will for you and me and every Christian, all the time.

His Promise

God has promised that he will always answer if we pray according to his will. "This is the confidence we have in approaching God: that if we ask anything according to his will, he hears us. And if we know that he hears us—whatever we ask—we know that we have what we asked of him" (1 John 5:14–15 NIV). What an amazing promise! God is telling us that there is one kind of prayer he will always answer with a yes. And what kind of prayer is that? How can we know in advance that God will answer yes? It's very simple. All we have to do is ask for something we know is God's will. And how can we know for sure a certain request is God's will? There is only one way to know for sure. God has to tell us. And in the case of being filled with the Spirit, God has already told us. God would never command us to do something that is against his will. God does not contradict himself! So if God has commanded us to be filled (and he has), and if we ask him to fill us, then he will. It's as simple as that.

Too Easy?

"Wait a minute," Nick said. "Go back over that again."

Sitting in our dorm room, Nick and I had reached the point in the blue booklet where it talked about God's command and promise. As I mentioned, Nick was an excellent student. But this simple concept seemed to baffle him. So we went over it again.

"Nick, do you sincerely want to be directed and empowered by the Holy Spirit?"

"Yes I do."

"And do you confess that you are a sinner?"

"Yes, of course. I've always known that."

"And do you accept Christ's death as forgiveness for all your sins?"

"Yes, I'm very grateful for the cross."

"Are you willing to give every area of your life over to God and let him change you any way he desires?"

Nick paused for a moment as if thinking hard.

"Yes, Alan, I really am."

"Well, Nick," I said, "it's clear to me that you meet all the prerequisites for being filled. So all that's left is to grab hold of his command and promise by faith."

Nick let out a long breath. "I know, and that's the part I just can't seem to get."

"Okay," I said. "Let's go over it again." I was pretty sure from his attitude it was not Nick's self-will that was getting in the way. I began to suspect spiritual warfare and shot up a silent prayer for protection against the powers of darkness.

"Nick, do you believe that God wants us to be filled with the Spirit?"

Nick paused. "Yes," he said slowly.

"How do you know he wants us to be filled?"

Nick paused again. It felt to me a little like trying to pull out a wisdom tooth, but I bit my tongue and waited for him to answer.

"Well, he says he wants us to be filled, right here in Ephesians." Nick pointed to the verse in the booklet.

"So would you say it is God's will that you be filled with the Spirit right now?"

"Uhh . . . I guess so, yes."

"How do you know?"

"Well, he commanded us to be filled and I guess he wouldn't command us to do something that wasn't in his will."

"Okay," I said, "so we've determined that it is God's will for you to be filled with the Spirit, right here, right now."

"Yes, that's right," he said.

"Now we're ready to look at the verses in 1 John." Nick read them out of the booklet.

"Nick, what do these verses say will happen when we ask according to God's will?"

"It says that he will hear us."

"That's right. And what will happen if he hears us?"

"It says he will give us what we ask."

"That's right. So, Nick, let me ask you. If you were to pray and ask God to fill you with the Spirit right now, would he do it?"

"Uhh . . . I'm not sure."

Nick must have seen the consternation on my face.

"Alan, I must just be a spiritual dodo. We can quit talking about this, if you want to."

"No, it's okay. Let's go back over it again."

And so together we read through the booklet a third time and then a fourth. Finally I saw the beginning of a smile on Nick's face.

"Let me make sure I've got it straight," he said finally. "These verses say that if I pray and ask God to fill me with the Holy Spirit, he will definitely do it. Is that right?"

"Exactly," I said, leaning back on the bed and relaxing a little.

"I understand it," he said slowly. "But somehow it just seems too easy."

"Let me ask you something," I said. "Is the gospel of salvation simple or complex?"

"I'm not sure what you mean."

"Is it simple enough for a child to understand it and receive Christ, for example?"

"I see what you mean," Nick said. "Pretty simple, I guess. My mom says I received Christ when I was four, though I don't remember it."

"Right," I agreed. "So God has made salvation so simple a four-year-old could understand it. Do you think he would then turn around and make the means to living the Christian life so complex only a Ph.D. could figure it out?"

"You're right, of course. I just don't understand how I missed it for so many years."

"I can't answer that," I said. "But I can see you get it now."

"Yes, I do."

Nick turned the page in the booklet and found the place where Bill Bright had written a suggested prayer. Nick began to read the prayer out loud.

Dear Father, I need You. I acknowledge that I have sinned against You by directing my own life. I thank You that You have forgiven my sins through Christ's death on the cross for me. I now invite Christ to again take His place on the throne of my life. Fill me with the Holy Spirit as

You commanded me to be filled, and as You promised in Your Word that You would do if I asked in faith. I pray this in the name of Jesus. As an expression of my faith, I now thank You for directing my life and for filling me with the Holy Spirit.[1]

Something in Nick's voice made me wonder.

"Nick, if you don't mind my asking, were you just reading that prayer or were you actually praying it?"

The little smile had returned. "I was praying it."

Now I was smiling. "So let me ask you, did God answer your prayer? Are you filled with the Holy Spirit?"

"How would I know? Am I supposed to feel something?"

"Not necessarily," I said. "But let me ask you the question. How can you know whether God has heard and answered your prayer?"

Nick's smile was growing.

"Because he promised to answer if I prayed according to his will."

"And did you pray according to his will?"

This time there was no hesitation. "Yes, I did."

"And so what did God do?"

"He filled me with his Spirit."

"Are you sure?" I asked.

"Yes, I am." By now the smile had grown to a grin.

"By Jove, I think he's got it," I said in a lousy imitation of Henry Higgins from *My Fair Lady*. Nick didn't seem to mind.

"Thanks, Alan. Thanks for hangin' in there with me. I wasn't sure I was ever going to understand."

"You're quite welcome," I said. "It's been a privilege to go through this with you."

Now I was grinning. "You know what I'm looking forward to?"

"No, what?"

"I'm looking forward to seeing what God does in your life during the rest of this school year."

"Me too," said Nick.

Spiritual Breathing

As I learned at that first Campus Crusade conference right after I'd become a Christian, Bill Bright developed an even simpler way of thinking about the Spirit-filled life. He calls it "spiritual breathing." It's a kind of shorthand for Christians who have already initially prayed to be filled with the Spirit. This was the first door through which I entered into an ongoing walk of faith. And it is still one I make use of frequently, along with several of the other doors we've discussed in previous chapters. Like physical breathing, spiritual breathing is an ongoing process that involves two parts, inhaling and exhaling.

Exhale

We exhale spiritually by confessing our sins. Confession simply means to agree with what God says about our sin. First, we must agree with God that our sin (in thought, word, or deed) was really wrong. No rationalizing allowed! But agreeing with God also means accepting Christ's death as the forgiveness and cleansing for our sins. By exhaling we get rid of the "bad air," any sin that is choking our walk with God.

Inhale

We inhale by surrendering control of our lives to Christ and receiving the fullness of the Holy Spirit by faith. Inhaling is an act of faith where we believe that we are filled based on his promise, whether we immediately feel or see any difference or not. When we inhale, we are filling our whole lives (not just our lungs) with the pure, refreshing "air" of the Holy Spirit.[2]

Physical versus Spiritual Breathing

Let me suggest some differences between physical and spiritual breathing. We must continually breathe physically every moment of our lives or we will quickly die. But spiritual breathing is only necessary when we intentionally sin. Being filled with the Spirit is the natural state of a Christian. Once we are filled with the Spirit, we will stay that way until we choose to disobey and take back the control of our lives through a conscious act of sin. When we sin intentionally, we need to breathe spiritually. How often will you need to breathe spiritually? The answer is as often as you sin! If you are having a difficult struggle with a recurring sin (say, impure thoughts), you may need to breathe spiritually more often than physically for a while. At the other end of the spectrum, I think it is thoroughly possible to go for days or even weeks when you are walking so closely with the Lord that spiritual breathing is not necessary for the whole period.[3]

Unknown Unrighteousness

Unintentional wrongdoing (such as honest mistakes, sins of omission, or immaturity) does not break our fellowship with God or hinder our Spirit-filled walk. If it did, no one could ever be Spirit-filled in this life, since even the most mature believers are continuing to grow in their understanding and application of God's absolute holiness. Technically, unrighteous behavior does not quench the filling of the Spirit, because long before we were born Christ died for all the sins we will ever commit. It is the attitude of faithlessness (rebellion, self-will, or disobedience) that breaks our fellowship with God and puts us back on the track toward worldly carnality. But what if the Holy Spirit shows us that something we did in the past was wrong, even though we were not aware it was wrong at the time? Does that mean we have not been filled with the Spirit ever since our unintentional wrongdoing? Not at all. If we agree with God quickly, our fellowship is unbroken. A Christian who is filled with the Spirit will say, "Thank you for showing me that what I did was wrong. Thank you that it too was forgiven by Christ's death. Give me the power never to do it again." That is the attitude of faith. If we respond that way, our walk with God is unbroken.

I believe the distinction between intentional and unknown sin is made by John in 1 John 1. In verse 7 John says, "If we walk in the light as He Himself is in the light, we have fellowship with one another, and the blood of Jesus His Son cleanses us from all sin." When John talks of "walking in the light," I believe he is speaking about what this door into faith calls "being filled with the Spirit" or "walking in the Spirit." John says that when we are walking in the light, the blood of Jesus continually cleanses us from all sin. But if we are filled with the Spirit, what sin does Jesus need to continue cleansing? Not our past intentional sins. Jesus' blood already cleansed those when we confessed them. The answer is our unknown unrighteousness. As Christians, we all have areas of imperfection, lack of conformity to God's perfect holiness. But much of this is not yet known to us. And yet it is sin. It involves areas where we still "fall short of the glory of God" (Rom. 3:23). I believe this is the kind of sin John is talking about in verse 7. If we are walking in the Spirit, by God's power staying free of intentional, known sin, then the blood of Christ continually cleanses us of the sins we don't yet know about.

Becoming His Witness

What about my roommate, Nick? Did learning how to be filled with the Spirit affect his fear of witnessing? First, let me say that walking in the Spirit did not change Nick's basic personality. He was still studious, hardworking, and disciplined. In fact a little bit of it even rubbed off on me. Often I'd come back from class only to find Nick already hitting the books at two in the afternoon. Out of respect for him, I tried to keep quiet in our shared, tiny room. Sooner or later, I'd run out of other distractions and have no other option but to study some myself!

But gradually I did see some changes in Nick. He began to be more honest in sharing his problems, not only with me but sometimes in our small-group Bible study. Occasionally when I was talking to nonbelievers in the cafeteria, Nick would toss in a few words of his own witness. The next year, when we were both seniors, he would sometimes tell of chances he'd have to speak up in class or bring up Christ in his assignments.

However, Nick's most dramatic opportunity came the week we all graduated. It was no surprise to me that Nick ended up with the highest grade point average in his entire division of the college (nearly a thousand students). Along with the other four students who were graduating at the top of their divisions, Nick was interviewed by one of the large local TV stations there in San Francisco. The year was 1969 and our campus was just one of many torn by months of violent confrontations between police and radical students. The mood among much of my graduating class was either pessimism or defiance.

The reporter posed the same question to each of the five students. "In light of what is happening in our country, what hope do you have for the future?" One of the students repeated some platitude about how he hoped the basic goodness of human nature would overcome all the violence and we could all learn to live together in peace. Several of the students were quite pessimistic and basically said they had no real hope for the future at all.

But I'll never forget Nick's answer. For some reason the TV station chose to put his on last. I was sitting in the dorm lounge with more than a hundred of my classmates watching the evening news. When Nick was asked about his hope for the future, he looked straight into the camera and spoke in a calm, clear voice. "Like many of my fellow students, when I look at recent events on my campus and in this country, I see no reason to hope at all." Nick paused briefly and then continued. "In fact the only reasons I have hope are the peace and love that have come into my life as the result of receiving Christ as my own personal Lord and Savior."

Without any further comment, the station went to commercial.

"You will receive power when the Holy Spirit comes on you; and you will be my witnesses . . . to the ends of the earth."

NINE

ENTER A CONSISTENT LIFE OF FAITH

J ohnny, can you tell us what the word *faith* means?" It was a cartoon I saw a number of years ago. Little Johnny was sitting in the front row of a Sunday school class.

"Faith," Johnny answered, "is trying to make yourself believe something you know isn't true."

Probably the cartoon was just meant to be funny, but as with much humor, part of what makes it funny is the element of truth behind the joke. Many people in Western culture today view faith as irrational. It's assumed that serious intellectuals, especially scientists, aren't going to believe in God or Christianity. And if you are a committed Christian, you must be some kind of ignorant yokel, or maybe you've just disconnected your brain. What's even more surprising is that many who consider themselves religious, or even Christians, think of faith pretty much the same way. Faith is emotional, irrational, or perhaps suprarational.

In this chapter I'm going to suggest what I think is a better and more biblical understanding of faith. I'm also going to explore why, even as Christians, we are often confused about the nature of faith. Then we're going to look back at each of our six doors and try to see how each, properly understood, can lead to true faith.

What Is Faith?

Believe it or not, I actually wrote my Ph.D. dissertation on the subject of this chapter—on the nature of faith. Don't worry, I'm not going to make you read any of my actual dissertation. However, I am going to share with you some of the conclusions I reached—without all the footnotes and fancy language.

To begin with, there is only one kind of Christian faith. The kind of faith that we exercise in initial salvation is exactly the same kind of faith we need to continue to exercise to have fellowship with and grow in our relationship with God. There is not one kind of faith that saves us and then some entirely different kind of faith that sanctifies us. There's not one faith that gets us into heaven and another that makes us holy. They are both the same kind of faith.

But what exactly is faith? After nearly a decade of research, I concluded that faith is *trust*. (I can just hear somebody thinking, *It took you ten years and a Ph.D. to figure that out?*) Well, there is a little more to it. Let me suggest a slightly fuller definition of faith.

Faith is when a person makes a commitment to another for an expected result. That is what I mean by trust. When I trust a person, I am committing myself to him or her (in a small or large way) with some expected result. It is not only possible to trust other people (and God), it is also possible to have faith (or trust) in things. The last time you drove a car or stepped into an elevator, you put your trust in a piece of machinery to take you where you wanted to go and not kill you in the process.

But I must admit that faith in God (at first glance, at least) seems to be a very different sort of trust than the trust I have in another human (or in my car). I think there is a difference, but the difference is not in the nature of the faith. Let me explain. What is the difference, for example, between trusting (or having faith in) my wife to make a deposit at the bank and trusting God to forgive my sins? There are, in my view, two important differences. One is the person in whom I'm placing my faith. In the case of my wife, I'm placing my faith in a very reliable woman of high intelligence who I know loves me. But she is also a fallible human being. Occasionally Jan gets busy or tired and forgets something. (I must admit, though, that she forgets things far less than I do!) When I put my faith in God, on the other hand, I'm trusting the omnipotent, omniscient, eternally faithful, immutable Creator and Sustainer of the universe. God cannot fail to do as he has promised. As trustworthy as Jan is, she occasionally fails. So the first difference between trusting Jan and trusting God is the nature of the object of my trust.

The other crucial difference is what I'm trusting them for. I am expecting a very different result from each of them. In the case of Jan's making a deposit, the result I'm expecting is that there will be more money in my account by evening (perhaps to cover a check I wrote today). But when I trust God to forgive my sins, the expected result is something of quite a different nature. If we are talking about my initial trust in God on the day I first received Christ, part of what I'm expecting as a result is that I will be freed from the penalty of eternal damnation. But let's say I'm talking about confessing my sins as a Christian. Then I'm trusting God for the result that my fellowship with him will be restored and that I will be filled with Christ and the power of the Holy Spirit. So one of the differences between my two examples of trust is the level of risk involved. One instance of faith may feel riskier than the other. I have to mention that there is an odd paradox about the risk component of trust. The paradox is that the risk can be high or low depending on whether we're talking about actual risk or perceived risk. Let me explain what I mean.

When I claim the promise of 1 John 1:9 and trust that God has forgiven my sins and restored me to fellowship, my actual risk is zero. God will always forgive and restore 100 percent of the time. But my feeling of risk may be fairly high. For example, when I broke a rule growing up, my father would say he forgave me. But then days or weeks later, he'd bring up my past behavior he'd supposedly forgiven. Then he'd yell at me and tell me what a bad kid I was because I was always doing that sort of thing. It may be very hard for me to really trust that God will forgive my confessed sin and never bring it up again. It may feel very risky to trust God, even though there is no actual risk at all.

So I have concluded that faith is trust, a commitment to another for an expected result.

Faith and Reason

"It's a mistake to try to prove the Bible or Christianity is true." A friend and I were sitting just outside a coffeehouse on a warm California evening two years ago.

I took a sip of cappuccino. "But the Bible and Christianity *are* true. Why would it be wrong to try to prove it?" I asked.

"The whole idea of proof is a product of the Enlightenment—one of the diseases of the modern era." Austin was a graduate student at a nearby seminary. Though he'd been a dedicated Christian for many years, recently he'd become fascinated with postmodernism. And now he was trying to convert me.

"Austin, I've always known that apologetic arguments don't appeal to everyone. But I think there are some non-Christians, and many Christians, who need to have their doubts and questions rationally answered before they can trust Christ and draw closer to him."

"It's a mistake, Alan. You're actually making it harder, not easier, for them to come to Christ or grow in him."

"So what would you do with nonbelievers or new believers who have serious doubts and aren't yet ready to trust Christ completely?"

"Just let them hang around committed Christians. I know you've heard the expression, 'Christianity is better caught than taught.' That's all I mean. Non-Christians and even many new believers are operating within a non-Christian worldview—an unbiblical web of meaning."

Austin took a bite of his pastry. "When you try to rationally translate Christian ideas like sin, grace, or forgiveness into their language and worldview, you just succeed in watering it down. Expose them to the real disease in its most virulent form. People are not reasoned into the kingdom, they're socialized into it."

I began this chapter by mentioning that many people today (even Christians like Austin) view faith as nonrational or even irrational. Actually that is only one of two mistakes that have been common in Christian circles for the last several hundred years. Unfortunately, both errors are still with us today. Some Christians see faith as an emotional preference that has nothing to do with reason or even goes contrary to reason. At the other end of the spectrum are some who see Christian faith as a list of doctrines to be believed. One group puts too much emphasis on reason, the other too little.

How did we get into this strange position of mass confusion by Christians over what faith really is? To answer that question, I'm going to need to take you on a whirlwind tour of some high points (or perhaps low points) of intellectual history during the past 350 years. But don't worry. I promise it won't hurt a bit! We're going to look at where these two competing ideas of faith came from.

Rational Faith

I want to begin our little historical tour about 350 years ago with British philosopher John Locke (1632–1704). Locke is probably most widely known for his general philosophical and political writings. But Locke also wrote two influential books where he talked about the nature of faith.[1]

For Locke faith was a belief based on revelation rather than reason alone. Locke held that some things (like the findings of science) could be proven on the basis of experience and reason. But on other matters, reason and experience do not help us. For these we must turn to a revelation that we have rationally concluded comes from God. Locke gives two examples: our knowledge of angels and our knowledge of resurrection. Our reason and experience give us no reliable information on either subject. But in the Bible we have a reliable revelation that tells us about both.[2] So when we accept what the Bible says about angels or the resurrection of Christ, our belief would be an example of what Locke calls "faith." So for Locke faith is nothing more or less than accepting ideas or concepts that come to us by means of revelation.

I want to make two crucial observations about Locke's understanding of faith. The first is that Locke puts reason above faith. Before we can have faith, our reason must determine that the source of the "revelation" is genuine. Locke thought it was rational to accept the Bible as a revelation from God, so it was rational to believe the statements in the Bible, even when they could not be independently tested by reason or experience. I also have a second comment to make about Locke's view of faith. For Locke, faith itself is something that happens in the mind. It is accepting certain things as true. Faith does not involve the emotions. It is not a choice of the will. Faith, for Locke, is only an event in the mind.

John Locke's idea of faith is important because his views influenced many of the Enlightenment thinkers who came along later, including Jean-Jacques Rousseau, David Hume, and Immanuel Kant. The big change these philosophers made was that they rejected revelation and made human reason the supreme (and often the only) judge of truth.[3] Largely through the pervasive influence of the Enlightenment, a rationalistic Locke-like view of faith has had many proponents in the nineteenth and twentieth centuries.[4]

In our coffeehouse conversation, Austin was objecting to modern evangelical ideas that have their root in and greatly resemble Locke's idea of faith. But what about Austin's own postmodern view of faith? Where did it come from? To understand Austin's view, we again need to journey back in history, though this time only about 150 years.

Radical Faith

Many today, both Christians and nonbelievers, see faith as a radical commitment that has little or nothing to do with reason. The one person who did the most to

popularize this view of faith was Danish philosopher
Søren Kierkegaard (1813–1855). Kierkegaard saw faith
as a passionate commitment filled with risk. In his view,
it was risky because it was contrary to reason. Kierkegaard
believed that the idea of God becoming a man in Christ
was totally against reason. He called it the Absolute Paradox.[5] Kierkegaard is the one who popularized the idea
of a "blind leap of faith." He thought evidences and
apologetic arguments for Christianity were the enemies
of faith. Kierkegaard influenced many twentieth-century thinkers, both secular and religious.[6] In addition,
some conservative and evangelical Christians have
adopted a Kierkegaard-like view of faith as a passionate
commitment.[7]

Relative Faith

One of the twentieth-century thinkers Kierkegaard
influenced was Ludwig Wittgenstein (1889–1951). Wittgenstein is considered the father of postmodernism and was
one of the thinkers who strongly influenced my friend
Austin. But while Kierkegaard and most of his existential
followers were individualistic, Wittgenstein stressed the
role a community plays in developing meaning. Kierkegaard believed an individual could have a life-changing
encounter with God, even if the surrounding society was
hostile or indifferent. But for Wittgenstein that kind of
individual experience of truth was impossible. In Wittgenstein's view, meaning is carried by language. And language is the carrier of the shared meaning of a community. I can no more have a private truth than I can have
a private language.

Austin took a sip of coffee. "Wittgenstein taught that
every language group on the face of the earth has its own
'web of meaning' bound up in and inseparable from the

language of that community. If you want to understand the shared meaning of a community, you must first learn its language."

"But wait a minute," I said. "That would mean you could never really translate the ideas of one community into another language."

"Not fully," Austin agreed.

"But don't some things translate 100 percent? How about when I point to the grass and say 'green' and my Latin American friend points to the same grass and says 'verde.' Don't we mean exactly the same thing in that case?"

"No," said Austin, "the two are not exactly identical, regardless of what your Spanish-English dictionary may say."

"But why not?"

"The Latin concept of verde is all tied up in Latin culture and experience. Even a simple idea like 'green' is bound up in an entire language and the community's experience that produced that language."

"So we're talking radical cultural relativity here, is that right?" I asked.

"Yes, I guess you could call it that."

"And what about the Christian community's concept of truth?"

"It's the same as any other. It's all bound up with the community's language and experience."

"So where does the truth that Christians believe come from?" I asked.

"It's just like the truth in any other community," Austin said. "Christian truth is produced over time by the Christian community."

"So Christian truth doesn't come primarily from God through the Bible?" I asked.

"Not in the top-down sort of way you mean it, no."

"Is God involved in Christian truth at all?"

"Well," Austin paused a moment. "That's an interesting question. Several of us evangelicals who are working in the Anglo-American postmodern movement are trying to figure out how to understand God's involvement. One suggestion is to see God himself as a member of the Christian community."

Can you begin to see the problems in defining faith as postmodernists do? What do we say to nonbelievers? We can't say Jesus is the Truth. In their language and its web of meaning, "truth" may be something entirely different than what we Christians mean. And what about reliable Bible translation? You can forget that! And can we even be sure that what we believe inside the Christian community is true? If God does not have any decisive role and is only a "participant" in the community, how can I be sure of anything?

Real Faith

Now, finally, after our little historical side trip, I'm ready to explain what I think is the real, biblical definition of faith. I'm convinced that true biblical faith involves both rational content and radical commitment. I do not believe that these two are warring alternatives (as they were for Locke, Kierkegaard, and so many since). Rather, I think rational content and radical commitment can be partners, two aspects of a unified whole. E. J. Carnell was on the right track when he said that faith is "a resting of the heart in the sufficiency of the evidences."[8] This definition brings together the idea of a heart commitment that is not at war with the reasoning of the mind but rests on the conclusions of the mind in sifting evidence. The primary adjustment I would make is to say that faith is a radical, total commitment of heart and life based on the rational conclusions of the mind. In Carnell's definition (and my adaptation of it), the heart and mind are not enemies. The mind can show that it is overwhelmingly probable that Christianity is true. On that basis the heart can take a leap of faith. But notice, it is not a blind leap, as in Kierkegaard. It is a leap based on knowledge and reason.

As I said earlier, the daily faith that is at the center of our walk as Christians is not a different type of faith than the faith that saves us. We are trusting the same Person (God), but for somewhat different results. In salvation I trust him to save me from punishment, to forgive my sins once and for all. I trust him to accept me into his family and change me. In my daily walk I trust him to direct me, to protect me, to provide for me, to answer my prayers, and so on. And there is always risk (or at least the feeling of risk) in my daily walk as well. Life in this fallen world seems to have an endless variety of challenges, temptations, and opportunities for growth. I believe this is part of God's providential design of life on earth.

Many times in this book I have brought up the idea that our Christian lives are a transition period similar to engagement. Why is it that many people go through doubts at some point during their engagement? It's because the idea of marriage can be scary. It is the unknown. We wonder, *Do I know this person well enough to trust her with my heart for the rest of my life? Is she safe? Will I still love her (and will she still love me) when we're forty or sixty or eighty?* Engagement can feel pretty risky and so can our walk with God.

You may have noticed by now that some of the doors into faith covered in this book have a more decisive quality and some seem more gradual. Both the brokenness and discipline doors emphasize process over event. The position, exchanged life, and grace doors have a more all-or-nothing quality about them. And the Spirit-filled door includes both initial and ongoing elements.[9] Of course, it's more complex than I've just made it sound. All the books I read in preparation for writing this book acknowledge the need to grow in our relationship with Christ. Even the positional truth and exchanged life authors gave some attention to the idea of gradual growth. And the opposite is also true. The brokenness and discipline writers recognize that there are certain decisive turning points in most Christians' walk with God.

I bring this up because, no matter what your favored door, it's important to recognize the valuable role of both crisis and continuity. Here is another way the doors can help balance each other. Some who enter through the more decisive doors get the impression that grasping your position or the Christ-life is the end goal of the Christian life. But properly understood, each of the doors is merely the means to a more consistent and deeper walk of faith. For believers who tend to look at their Christian life in black-white, either-or terms, the practice of the disciplines or making peace with God's long-range program of brokenness can be an effective antidote to superspiritual tendencies. Likewise if a believer tends to get bogged down in the process of the disciplines or brokenness, some time focusing on grace or the Christ-life can be a refreshing reminder that the Christian life is not about us or our progress but about a joyful relationship with a living God.

All I Know

Let me see if I can bring everything I've said in this book so far down into one simple and memorable phrase. I'm afraid I'm not creative enough to come up with something completely original. But I did hear such a statement many years ago. The statement is this. "Faith is giving as much of yourself as you know to as much of God as you know."[10] That really captures what I mean by trust. When I first became a Christian at age nineteen, I didn't really know myself all that well. And I certainly didn't know that much about God. But when I first learned how to be filled with the Spirit, I gave everything I was aware of to God as I understood him at the time. Now, thirty-five years later, I understand more about both the wonder of God's creation of me and my utter sinfulness without Christ. And I've also learned much about God's holiness, mercy, wisdom, and love.

The more I learn about God's character and the more I learn about my own gifts, calling, and weaknesses, the more I have to commit to God in faith. The faith itself does not change. It is still the same act of giving my whole self over to him. However, the realms in which I am able (and responsible) to exercise my faith have grown greatly over time.

Doors into Faith

"Dr. Scholes, I have a problem with this whole 'doors into faith' idea." I had been presenting the basic concepts of this book to one of my classes of seminary students. Joel, one of the brightest students in the class, had raised his hand.

"What's the problem?" I asked.

"How did you decide that faith was at the center and these other six biblical concepts were doors into it? I mean, why couldn't you say that faith is a door into the Spirit-filled life or a door into grace?"

As he often did, Joel had raised a crucial question.

There are two primary reasons why I consider faith as the central means to the Christian life. The first and most important reason is that I think the Bible gives faith the most central place when talking about how we are to approach God in living with him on this earth. God has said that "without faith it is impossible to please Him" (Heb. 11:6). In Romans, Paul tells us "everything that does not come from faith is sin" (Rom. 14:23 NIV). Faith is one of the themes that unifies the Old and New Testaments. The prophet Habakkuk declares, "The righteous will live by their faith" (Hab. 2:4 NLT). It's interesting that both Paul and the writer to the Hebrews quote this exact statement (Rom. 1:17; Gal. 3:11; Heb. 10:38). Whole books of the Bible center on the theme of faith, including Joshua, Romans, Galatians, and Hebrews. None of the individual doors is given so central a place by the Bible.[11]

The second reason I put faith in the center is that the idea of faith can tie all the doors together. It is a common denominator present in each of the doors.[12] In fact in the next chapter I will argue that if faith is missing from any of the doors, they no longer work. Without faith, none of the doors lead into a consistent walk with God.

I'd like to take a moment to look back at each of the doors. Let's see how faith is involved and how, properly understood, each door leads to an attitude of faith.

Position in Christ

It takes faith to believe I am seated in the heavenlies with Christ. This is especially true when other people treat me like dirt or when Satan accuses me in my mind. When I choose to live like a child of the King, I am trusting that what God says is truer than my own intuitions or what I see. I'm choosing to live the most holy life I can, in a manner fitting a child of the King.

Death to Self

When I come to the place that I can humbly accept the most hurtful experiences in life—when I can see them as allowed by the loving hand of God for my good—that is true faith. Rebellion, resistance, or trying to flee the pain—all of these are the opposite of faithful submission. The path of brokenness leads me to discover many new things about myself and about God, and opens new realms in which I can trust him.

Under Grace

As long as I am trying to earn God's favor, as long as I am trying to be good enough to please him, then I have not yet reached the attitude of faith. Faith says, "I accept your love even though I am unworthy." It takes true faith to believe that God is pleased with us no matter what we do. The more I understand my unworthiness, the more I can appreciate his grace.

Exchanged Life

It takes faith to believe that Christ is actually living in and through me. It often looks and feels like it is still the same old me living my life. To just quit my self-effort and trust the power of Christ in me, that is true faith. As I grow in my knowledge of myself and my knowledge of Christ, the contrast becomes clearer and I am able to open myself more broadly to the control from his life within me.

Disciplined Life

Godly discipline requires faith. When I fail over and over, only faith allows me to get up and try again. True discipline requires an attitude of faith every day, every hour (and sometimes every minute). As I practice the disciplines, I gain greater knowledge of my own rebellious and undisciplined nature. I also gain a truer and clearer vision of the holiness and beauty of God.

Spirit Filled

We are filled with the Spirit by faith. We breathe spiritually as an act of faith. We do not depend on our feelings to know we are filled, rather we trust (have faith in) the promise of God's Word. As the Holy Spirit gradually reveals new areas of sinfulness, we expand the Spirit's influence in our lives.

I hope it's clear how each of the doors, properly understood, requires faith to open and leads to an attitude of faith on the other side. Each of the doors truly opens only with an attitude of faith. When Christians try to use the doors with a different attitude, what they find is not faith but something else. In the next chapter we will begin to look at what believers find instead, when the doors are misunderstood or misused.

TEN

ALMOST FAITH

Four Common Confusions

During the past thirty-five years I've met many sincere believers who have genuinely desired to walk closely with God but were frustrated. Their agony is the primary reason I've written this book. These believers usually were exposed to at least one of the doors into faith. But it was not working for them. Why? I wondered. I believe the answer is that there are a number of common confusions about faith. Many of these sincere Christians have been trying to enter by one of the doors but have been missing the true attitude of faith. They are caught in one of the forms of what I call "almost faith."[1] Let's look at four of these common confusions in some detail.

Lost in Legalism—The Effort Error

"Alan, it all just seems so hopeless."

Our Christian education meeting had just broken up. Brianna had been unusually quiet. Her dark eyes seemed moody, withdrawn. I'd asked her if she wanted to go across the street and get a frozen yogurt before heading home. Brianna was one of those tireless church workers that everyone wanted on his or her committee. I was delighted when she agreed to sit on the one I chaired. I'd been in the church only a couple of years, but I already knew if you want it done, give it to Brianna. She'll do it right and usually before the deadline. I knew she served on several other committees, taught Sunday school, volunteered at the homeless shelter, all on top of taking care of two little kids of her own. But now she looked exhausted and lifeless as she toyed with her granola-covered, fat-free yogurt.

"I've got a great life and I know I shouldn't complain. I'm married to a wonderful man. He works hard to take care of me and the kids." A faint smile crossed her face. "He's with them now. He always takes them on Sundays when I have meetings—which is just about every Sunday."

"So what is it, Brianna? Obviously something's wrong."

She swirled her yogurt some more, mixing in the granola. It was starting to melt and it didn't look like she was going to eat any of it.

"You remember last week when the pastor said God was pleased with us, just because we're his children?"

"Yes, I do," I said.

"I wish I could believe that, but it sure doesn't feel that way. Maybe if I were a better Christian. Maybe if I spent more time in prayer or could go on one of those short-term missions to Venezuela or Guatemala. 'Cept I don't know what I'd do with the girls; Kyle has to work and . . ."

"Wait!" I said. "I don't know anyone who serves the Lord as diligently as you. I don't think a mission trip is the answer."

"Then what is?" Her voiced sounded tortured.

"Tell me about your family, your parents I mean."

"Oh, you don't want to hear about them. There's really not much to tell."

"Sure I do. Tell me about your dad. What was he like?"

It seemed that Brianna's eyes looked even sadder, if that were possible.

"Oh, Dad was from the old school. He was an engineer, a retired marine. He ran our household like we were all in basic training. 'A tight ship,' that's what he used to call our home."

"And what about your mother?"

"She was quiet and did what he told her—we all did. Especially me. I was the oldest of four so he expected a lot of me. And, really, I'm grateful. That's where I learned high standards and how to work hard."

"And what did your dad say when you had done a job well?"

"Ha," she said with a derisive tone. "We never found out."

"You mean you never lived up to his standards?"

Brianna paused, thinking.

"No, that's not quite true. On rare occasions he would simply say nothing. I guess we all knew that meant we'd done okay."

"But most of the time?"

"Most of the time he'd point out how we could have done it better or faster or more efficiently. And he was right; usually there were ways we could improve."

Brianna was suffering from what I call "almost faith" in one of its most pervasive and insidious forms, legalism. As we talked further, I learned that Brianna had been taught the discipline door as the way to live the Christian life.

From an early age she regularly had a quiet time, prayed, studied, memorized, fasted, and served. She had been taught that she must yield every area of her life to God and for years sincerely had tried to do so. But Brianna was certain her yielding was incomplete and immature so she never believed God could accept her. She always seemed to hear the voice of God speaking with the authoritarian tones of her father.

The Bible has a lot to say about legalism. We've already looked at much of that teaching when we talked about the Grace door. Some of what the Bible says about legalism is talking about nonbelievers (like many Jews in the first century) who are trying to earn God's favor by what they do. But it is also clear that this was (and is) a problem for those who already know Christ. Many in the Galatian church were legalistic believers who were missing a true walk of faith. Paul uses pretty strong language to try to knock them out of their legalism: "You foolish Galatians, who has bewitched you . . . ? This is the only thing I want to find out from you: did you receive the Spirit by the works of the Law, or by hearing with faith? Are you so foolish? Having begun by the Spirit, are you now being perfected by the flesh?" (Gal. 3:1–3). The Galatians had accepted Christ and been indwelt by the Holy Spirit by faith. But now they were trying to live the Christian life in their own power on the basis of their own hard work.

In over thirty years of ministry I have discovered two very different types of legalists. The Galatians represent one sort of legalist and Brianna is an example of the other. The Galatians' problem was pride; Brianna's was discouragement and defeat.

We've already seen how Paul dealt with the proud Galatians. His words echo the way Jesus often tore into the proudly legalistic Pharisees. But God's attitude toward the broken and exhausted is quite different. Those like Brianna who have worked so hard and fear they will never be good enough need gentle encouragement. "Encourage the exhausted, and strengthen the feeble. Say to those with anxious heart, 'Take courage, fear not'" (Isa. 35:3–4). Paul tells the Thessalonians to "encourage the fainthearted, help the weak, be patient with all men" (1 Thess. 5:14).

Legalism is the attempt to please God or earn his approval through our own efforts. It is most common for those who have been taught or have tried to enter the Christian walk through the Death to Self or the Disciplined Life doors. But it is actually a misunderstanding of the biblical teaching regarding brokenness and discipline. An excellent way to counter the effort error is by studying and applying one of the more positive doors, such as grace or the Spirit-filled life.

Withering in Worthlessness—Difficulties with Self-Acceptance

"I've made such a mess of my Christian life." Richard slumped back into the chair. "I know I should get out of the way and let Christ live through me but I find it hard to do. Occasionally, when something goes really well, I can see that Christ must have taken over. But most of the time, I get in the way and things are hard or don't turn out the way they should. I often feel like God's kingdom would get along better if I were not a part of it!"

Richard suffers from a sense of worthlessness. The belief we are worthless to God is a debilitating half-truth that keeps many from a genuine walk of faith.

Let me see if I can simplify the biblical teaching about humanity down to its most basic form. The Bible tells us two things about the human race. It says that we are wonderfully made and hopelessly fallen. I sometimes call this the good news and bad news about us.[2] In the very beginning of the Bible we find the wondrous story of creation.

God created heaven and earth, day and night, plants and animals. Then he paused to consider his work in progress "and God saw that it was good" (Gen. 1:25). Following that, God made men and women in his own image and put them in charge of everything else he had made on the planet. Then he stopped again to consider all he'd made and this time he saw "it was very good" (Gen. 1:31). What changed God's evaluation of his creation from "good" to "very good"? Only one thing was added—us, the human race.

Ah, I can just hear some Christians saying, "But that was before the fall." They're right. It was. Some think that after the fall, we became worthless—that the image of God was erased from humanity. They think we became lower than dog dung, a blight on the planet.

But it is not true that the fall made us worthless. The Bible does not teach that we lost the image of God when we fell. David says, "I praise you because I am fearfully and wonderfully made; your works are wonderful" (Ps. 139:14 NIV). God forbids murder and also verbal abuse because even non-Christians retain a significant image of God (Gen. 9:6; James 3:9). So every human being, even though fallen, has great worth as God's special creation.

As Christians we have a second reason to see ourselves as valuable. Christ has not only forgiven us but given us a new life and a new position of honor in the church, his body (2 Cor. 5:17; 1 Cor. 12:22–24). God sees us as valuable, not worthless. How dare we not accept ourselves when God himself has accepted us?

Missing the true attitude of faith through problems of self-acceptance is most common in those who try to enter through the Exchanged Life, Death to Self, or Disciplined Life doors. Some misunderstand the Exchanged Life door as Richard did. They get the idea that all they are good for is to get out of the way so that Christ can live through them. They try to become empty tubes, so that God can be everything and they can be nothing.

The problem is God didn't go to all the trouble of making you so that you could turn around and become nothing. God plans to make you much more than you are, not less.

Perhaps I need to clarify something that may be bothering you. The Bible does say that Christ humbled himself, becoming a servant and that we are to follow his example (Phil. 2:3–8). Jesus said, "Anyone who wants to be the first must take last place and be the servant of everyone else" (Mark 9:35 NLT). The problem these passages are trying to correct is actually opposite to the problem of worthlessness. There are many in the world, including many Christians, who hunger for positions of authority over others. They want power and privilege. God's message to them is, "First learn to be a servant." But a servant is not nothing. Particularly, being a servant of a king is an important role. The problem with power-hungry or proud believers is not that they see themselves as valuable. Their problem is that they see themselves as more important than they should. Notice the exact way Paul words his warning to the Roman Christians. "I say to every man among you not to think more highly of himself than he ought to think; but to think so as to have sound judgment" (Rom. 12:3). Paul is not saying the Romans should see themselves as worthless. They are to realistically evaluate their own worth and not exaggerate their importance in their own eyes.

True faith does not mean viewing ourselves as worthless. Rather, it means having a realistic view of ourselves, which is neither too high nor too low. In both the act of creation and our re-creation in Christ, God himself has asserted his approval of our intrinsic worth. True faith involves accepting our created worth, our gifts and calling, and being confident and content in the positions and roles God gives us.

This afternoon, shortly after I typed the last paragraph, I received tragic news. A wonderful Christian man whom I had known for more than a quarter century had committed suicide. Harry was my disciple during his college years. I encouraged him to enter full-time Christian ministry. My wife and I counseled Harry and his bride-to-be during their courtship.

Harry struggled his whole Christian life with feelings of worthlessness, inadequacy, and depression. On many occasions during his college years and since, I had tried to encourage him with the message of the love and grace of God. In recent years he lived half a continent away and the last time we spoke was more than a year ago. Now my dear brother Harry had lost the struggle and my heart grieved for him.

Sometimes a sense of worthlessness can be a matter of life and death.

Lolling in License—Missing God's Holiness

The chairman of the deacon board sat in the front pew, looking like someone had just punched him in the stomach. His sixteen-year-old daughter, Jennifer, stood at the microphone and spoke to the congregation.

"Thanks, so much, for giving me and all the other kids scholarships to go to the youth conference. There was this great speaker! He told us how we don't have to read our Bibles or pray or witness or obey rules and stuff—'cause Jesus loves us just the way we are!"

I feel some kinship with Jennifer, the deacon's daughter. When I miss the true attitude of faith, it is usually through an attitude of license. License is taking God's holiness lightly. License says, "Well, God loves me and I'm filled with the Spirit, so it doesn't really matter that much what I do."

Like Brianna, some of my error with regard to faith can probably be traced to my upbringing and Christian experience. As I said earlier, during most of my growing-up years, my dad was busy with work and emotionally distant from me. My mother, on the other hand, was a stay-at-home mom and spent lots of time with me. Though she was a loving and consistent parent, she was also a lenient one. Like most children, I formed an unconscious view of God from the attitudes of my parents toward me. The God-image that came from my dad was a distant and indifferent God. From Mom it was a loving and tolerant God.

The first two doors into faith I was exposed to were the Spirit Filled door and the Under Grace door. These both seemed natural to me, since I could easily see that God loved me unconditionally (like Mom) and wasn't terribly concerned with the letter of the law (my exact behavior) like my dad. I'm not saying I was consciously aware that I was transferring my parents' attitudes to God. I did not realize I had done that until many years later. But how I experienced God's attitude toward me was a combination of the attitudes I'd experienced growing up.

I think there was another factor that fed into license being my "error of choice." By personality I am an optimist. I usually believe the best of people and expect things to turn out pretty well in my life. I'm not generally given to suspicion or worry. So it was easy to expect that God would love me and take care of me.

License, taking God's moral laws and holiness lightly, is a misunderstanding of faith common for those trying to enter through the Under Grace and Spirit Filled doors. And it truly is a misunderstanding of faith. Both Paul and James argue that real faith will result in good works, not immorality (Rom. 6:1–4; James 2:17–26).

Stranded by Super-Spirituality—Maintaining an Illusion

"Don't talk to me about the secret to a life of faith." Kimber's tone was sullen and sarcastic. "I went to all those seminars when I was a new Christian. I read the books and heard the talks. 'The abundant life,' 'spiritual power,' 'living above my circumstances.' I heard it all and I tried it all. And let me tell you something; it doesn't work, none of it! My life got worse, not better. I got misery, not happiness. Maybe those formulas work for some people, but not for me."

Kimber is suffering from a misunderstanding of faith I call "super-spirituality." Super-spirituality is the concept that once you've learned the "secret," you've "arrived" and should have no more problems or trials. This confusion is most common with those trying to enter a life of faith through the Spirit Filled, Position in Christ, or the Exchanged Life doors. Some who are told about being filled with the Spirit get the message that the Holy Spirit will make them feel good all the time. Some misunderstand the teaching about position to mean that we will live completely above our circumstances and not be affected by our everyday problems and trials. Some think the exchanged life should be one with no difficulties. Sometimes the problem originates with overzealous teachers who tout the benefits of their door with superlatives and don't balance their teaching with the rest of what the Bible says about the Christian life.

Yes, Jesus did say "I came that they might have life, and might have it abundantly" (John 10:10). He did say, "Take My yoke upon you. . . . For My yoke is easy, and My load is light" (Matt. 11:29–30). But that is not all he said to his followers.

Once someone told Jesus, "I will follow you no matter where you go" (Luke 9:57 NLT). How did Jesus respond?

Did he promise the man land, a mansion, and servants? No, instead Jesus gave him a warning. "Foxes have dens to live in, and birds have nests, but I, the Son of Man, have no home of my own, not even a place to lay my head" (v. 58 NLT). But perhaps Jesus' most sweeping and frightening promise to his disciples is that they will be hated.

> When the world hates you, remember it hated me before it hated you. The world would love you if you belonged to it, but you don't. I chose you to come out of the world, and so it hates you. Do you remember what I told you? "A servant is not greater than the master." Since they persecuted me, naturally they will persecute you. And if they had listened to me, they would listen to you! The people of the world will hate you because you belong to me, for they don't know God who sent me.
>
> John 15:18–21 NLT

Jesus' early disciples understood the Christian life was not easy or trouble free. James writes, "Consider it all joy, my brethren, when you encounter various trials, knowing that the testing of your faith produces endurance" (James 1:2–3). Sooner or later, every Christian will face trials of one kind or another. Paul writes to his disciples about his own trials and about theirs. "For just as the sufferings of Christ are ours in abundance, so also our comfort is abundant through Christ. . . . knowing that as you are sharers of our sufferings, so also you are sharers of our comfort" (2 Cor. 1:5, 7).

The truth is that walking in faith does not reduce our trials or problems but rather gives us new resources to deal with them. Properly understood, being Spirit filled, knowing my position in Christ, or relying on the life of Christ within me will not insulate me from trials or sorrows. Rather, I now have the supernatural power of God available to me to meet trials and challenges that would have destroyed me had I tried to face them alone.

Do you like adventure movies? Action films? I do. But let me ask you a question. Would you be willing to put yourself in the shoes of Indiana Jones, especially if you didn't know for sure there would be a happy ending? Do you really want to be shot at with poisoned arrows, thrown in a snake pit, or dragged behind a car? Most of us prefer to experience adventures like those vicariously in a darkened theater.

God intends the Christian life to be an adventure no less exciting. Sometimes God actually does call believers to face physical danger, but more often we are asked to risk ridicule, misunderstanding, or just the heroic, quiet, daily struggle against sin.

But we face these trials with resources greater than even the movie heroes. First, we have the confidence of knowing we are on the side of the living God who made, knows, and can control everything. And second, we know there will be the happiest of all possible endings, whether we live or whether we die.

We are right when we tell non-Christians or new believers that the Christian life can be a great adventure. But we must also warn them that it is an adventure filled with risk, trial, and possibly even suffering.

From Almost to Real Faith

Most of us lean toward one or more of these four ways of misunderstanding or missing an attitude of faith. But sometimes one person may suffer from more than one of these spiritual afflictions. I suspect that Brianna, the diligent church worker, was not only caught up in legalism but was also finding it difficult to accept herself and see herself as valuable to God. Let me suggest three possible solutions you can try if you find yourself frequently missing faith through one or more of these confusions.

The first suggestion is to study Scripture passages that are a natural counter to your error. If you're like me and lean toward license, spend some time reading the Old Testament prophets or other passages that serve as windows into God's holiness and attitude toward sin. If you struggle with feelings of worthlessness, study the sections of Psalms or Paul's letters that speak about the value God places on all humans and particularly on believers.

The second suggestion is to spend time exploring doors that are very different from your natural personality bent. If you tend toward super-spirituality, spend time working on some of the godly disciplines to gain a vision of how far you have yet to grow. If legalism tends to trip you up, study the grace door or the Spirit-filled life.

The third suggestion is to consciously seek out believers who are different in temperament or background and who naturally gravitate toward different doors (or lean toward opposite errors). Time in fellowship, study, prayer, and especially mutual accountability will go a long way toward helping you move from "almost faith" to a life of more consistent trust.

For most of my adult life I've been involved with some kind of small accountability group or another. During the majority of our more than thirty years of marriage, Jan and I have been in church-based small groups together. Every Tuesday morning for the past several years, I've gotten up early to meet with my Promise Keepers' men's group. We have breakfast together, we share our joys and struggles, we encourage, and, when necessary, we exhort, and we always pray for each other. For me these intimate kinds of small groups help keep me from extremes in my Christian life. When I'm struggling, there's always a brother who's had a good week to encourage me. When things are going well, there's usually someone who needs my compassion and my prayers.

When I heard the news of Harry's suicide last night, the first person I called was one of the men in my Promise Keepers' group. We talked and prayed together and I hung up the phone with a renewed perspective. I have confirmed in my own experience the Bible's wise counsel. "Let us not give up meeting together, as some are in the habit of doing, but let us encourage one another" (Heb. 10:25 NIV).

ELEVEN

SIX SUGGESTIONS ABOUT FAITH

Don't Sit Outside and Look at the Doors!

I have a confession to make (another one!). One of the reasons I waited so long to write this book was that I was concerned that, for some people, the result might be more damage than benefit. It's been my privilege for many years to teach a doctrine survey class to many of the new Campus Crusade for Christ staff members as a part of their initial ministry training. For a few years in the 1980s, I included a session on these six doors into faith. But after I'd done it for a while, I decided it was not such a good idea. Most of these staff were in their early and mid-twenties. Some of them were fairly new believers, only a few years old in the Lord (as I had been when I joined CCC).

I realized that for these younger believers it was most important that they master one of the doors into faith and begin to use it consistently. There would be plenty of time later in their ministry career to discover the other doors.

Therefore, I have some concerns about writing this book and turning it loose on the Christian public. I'm concerned, especially for younger believers, that reading this book might lead to pride and a sense of intellectual superiority. Paul warned the Corinthians, "Knowledge makes arrogant, but love edifies" (1 Cor. 8:1). The point of understanding any of the doors is to actually enter and consistently walk in faith. It is better to concentrate on one door and actually enter than to know many doors in theory but never walk through any of them! So please, if you are a new believer, or an older believer who's never had a consistent walk of faith, I beg you: Choose a door and master it!

Don't Make Everyone Enter by Your Door

"The key to living the Christian life, the secret of experiencing God's power in your life, is understanding and living in light of your position in Christ." The speaker ended his talk, acknowledged the applause of the audience, and stepped down from the podium. Thirty or forty people, anxious to ask questions, immediately surrounded him.

This had been the last in a series of messages the speaker had given as a guest lecturer for one of Campus Crusade's senior staff training conferences. As I looked around the auditorium, I could see that most of the nearly one thousand present were full-time Crusade staff who had been in ministry for many years. As CCC staff they had all been exposed to the Spirit-filled door into faith. And my educated guess was that for at least 90 percent of them, it was the door they had first learned and the one they had used for most of their Christian lives.

However, this speaker had concentrated his whole series of messages on the Position in Christ door. He'd told how he'd lived for many years as a Christian layman in frustration and defeat. Then he'd learned the secret—his position in Christ. In recent years he'd begun a ministry of speaking and writing. In all his talks and books he stressed the importance of Christians knowing and appropriating their lofty position as children of the King.

I noticed a friend of mine, a successful campus director from another state. The look on his face was one of frustration and concern. Finally, it was his turn to ask a question.

"I want to be sure I didn't misunderstand you," my friend began. "It sounded to me like you were saying a Christian couldn't have real spiritual power unless he understood his position in Christ."

"That's right. You understood me correctly."

"Okay. What I'm wondering is this." The Campus Crusade veteran held up a copy of Bill Bright's little blue booklet, "Have You Made the Wonderful Discovery of the Spirit-Filled Life?"

"Are you familiar with this booklet?" my friend asked.

"Yes," said the speaker. "I've read it and I think I have a good grasp of what it says."

"Let's say," said my friend, "that a new believer reads this booklet, understands it, and sincerely does what the booklet suggests, prays in faith to be filled with the Spirit. But this new believer has never heard or read any teaching about his position in Christ."

"Okay," the speaker nodded, "I understand the hypothetical."

My friend got a kind of steely glint in his eye.

"What I'm wondering is whether you think this new believer could really have the fullness of God's power, just

through understanding and receiving the filling of the
Spirit by faith. Or do you think he would also have to first
learn about his position before he could really serve and
obey God?"

"The latter," the speaker said without hesitation. "Even
if he understood and applied what's in that booklet, he'd
still need to grasp his position in Christ to really experience the victorious Christian life."

It's clear to me our guest speaker spread a lot of confusion that day. In his own life the speaker had followed an
almost classic pattern. He'd become a Christian. Then he'd
spent a number of years in spiritual defeat and frustration.
Then he'd discovered one of the doors into faith. Almost
immediately his life had changed for the better. He felt
closer to God. He experienced victory over sin. His prayer
life and understanding of the Bible improved. He saw fruit
in evangelism. Then he began to share his discovery with
others, first one-on-one, then with larger and larger
groups. He had many people tell him their lives were transformed by this new truth, just as his had been. Then he
wrote training manuals and even published books. Each
was filled with anecdotes from his own life and those his
ministry had helped.

The central problem with this common career path in
ministry is that it is self-confirming. Many people are simply carried away by the enthusiasm of the speaker. Others who've been living in defeat are genuinely helped.
Those are the ones who usually seek out the speaker or
write letters with glowing reports of how this new truth
has changed their lives. But let me tell you what I know
is happening behind the scenes. Many who come to the
seminars or read the books are not helped. The door just
doesn't appeal to them. Others get excited by the door and
try to use it for a little while, but soon it doesn't work for
them and they return to a life of quiet unbelief. Usually
these people do not come up after meetings or write let-

ters. Often they assume there must be something wrong with them. And even when a speaker hears an occasional negative report, it is easily dismissed. "They didn't really understand" or "They're unteachable." After all, for every one who doesn't seem to "get it," there are dozens of stories of those the speaker has helped.

What is the problem here? I think it is natural to assume that everybody is just like us. When God has wonderfully changed us, it is a normal and even healthy instinct to want to share what we've discovered with others. The danger is when we insist that everyone must duplicate our own spiritual history. It is a kind of one-size-fits-all approach to the Christian life.

If there really was one (and only one) key to walking with God, why doesn't the Bible make it clear? And why are the other biblical doors present in Scripture? And why have so many godly Christian leaders entered through a variety of different doors?

Occasionally this kind of myopia about how to live the Christian life can lead to results that are almost funny. Sitting on my bookshelf is a wonderful little book called *The Sound of God's Applause: Living a Life That Glorifies the Father.*[1] In it pastor and professor Les Hughes contrasts what the Bible says about living in the fear of man with a life directed toward pleasing God, as Jesus did. Sitting right next to this book on my shelf are two books by Pastor Steve McVey.[2] I quoted one of them earlier in this book when I was discussing the grace door. In both books pastor McVey tells of years in ministry where he got up each morning asking God how he could please him today. What McVey was doing is almost word for word what Hughes says we should do. But for McVey the result was legalism. In McVey's testimony the "before" sounds an awful lot like Hughes's "after."

So is one of them wrong? I don't think so. Hughes is, I believe, describing what is for him and many others, a true walk of faith. For Hughes it was liberating to stop seeking the approval of men and start looking to God as his audience. But for McVey the very same idea, that he needed each day to perform for God as his audience, led to the misunderstanding of legalism. Not until McVey discovered the grace door could he actually enter a true walk of faith.

So that is another reason we should be careful not to make everyone else enter through our door. The same door that is life-giving for us can be deadening to someone else. We need to leave room for God to be original in the lives of his other children. If we are truly walking by faith, we will be quick to love and slow to judge other believers who are sincerely trying to live the Christian life, even if they are entering through a door that does not feel natural to us.

I mentioned in the acknowledgments that one of the things that got me started thinking about doors into faith was the gracious attitude of Bill Bright. On many occasions over the past thirty years, I've listened as Bill warmly introduced a distinguished pastor or Christian leader from a ministry outside of Campus Crusade. And fairly frequently these speakers have then taught about the Christian life in ways that were quite different from Bill's own emphasis on walking in the Spirit. The first time it happened I held my breath. Would Bill get up after the speaker and denounce him as a heretic? Or would he just gently try to balance the man's words, perhaps on a later occasion? To my surprise he did neither. Instead, when the guest was finished, Bill came to the microphone and praised the words of the guest speaker and heartily encouraged all the CCC staff to put his teaching into practice!

Focus on One of the Doors

"I don't teach the Spirit-filled life anymore." Emily was a mother of three and a long-time staff member with Campus Crusade. She'd asked to talk with me after one of the sessions of a summer class I was teaching to veteran staff workers.

"As a new believer, I learned to walk in the Spirit. It was wonderful and liberating! But now, twenty years later, it's just gotten to be a ritual—I feel like I'm just going through the motions. It often seems like God is very far away."

"I don't think your experience is all that unusual," I said.

Emily looked surprised. Then she continued. "A few months ago, I went to a seminar where the speaker taught about our position in Christ. It has changed my life! I feel more excited about my walk with the Lord than I have in years!"

"I'm glad," I said. "But I don't understand why you've stopped teaching about being filled with the Spirit."

"For many years, I've led a women's Bible study for new believers. And until recently I've always made it a priority to help women learn about the Spirit-filled life early in their Christian experience. But I don't do that anymore. Now I concentrate on telling them about positional truth."

"Why?"

"Because it's revolutionary—it's changed my life."

"Wait a minute," I said. "When you were a baby believer, didn't you think the ministry of the Spirit was revolutionary—didn't it change your life?"

"Yes, but . . . hmm. I think I see where you're going."

"One of the dangers of being in the ministry for a long time is that we begin to share what we're currently interested in with our disciples. Sometimes it's what we need but not what they need."

"I think I see," she said. "But I don't understand why being filled with the Spirit used to be so great and isn't anymore."

"If you have a little time, I'd like to show you a concept that I think will help put all this into perspective."

"Okay."

I spent the next half hour showing Emily the six doors into faith.

"Wow," she said when I was finished. "This really makes sense. As a new Christian I was going through the Spirit-filled door, but over time it just became a mechanical ritual and I started missing the real attitude of faith."

"That's right," I said.

"And then I learned about the position door and, because it was fresh and new, I began to really walk in faith again."

"That's what it sounds like to me."

Emily was quiet for a moment, obviously thinking it through.

"So you think I should go back to sharing the Spirit-filled door with my women?"

"Yes, I do."

"But why not start them on the position door or one of these others you've shown me?"

"I can think of several reasons," I said.

"Such as?"

"With a new believer, or anyone who is not already walking consistently with the Lord, I think it's most helpful to concentrate on one of the doors to begin with. Our first steps of faith can be scary and confusing enough, without complicating it by presenting several doors."

"That makes sense," she said. "But why start with the Spirit-filled door?"

"In your case, I'd start there because you are a part of a movement. Loyalty is one issue. That is the door this movement has emphasized. But there are practical reasons. Your women are most likely to spend time with other believers in the CCC ministry. Their walk of faith will be reinforced by other Christians who are understanding and talking about faith in the same way."

"And if I wasn't on Crusade staff, what would you tell me?"

"That depends," I said. "If you were part of another ministry that emphasized a particular door, I'd encourage you to lead with that door. If you were a Navigator, for example, I would tell you to start with the Disciplined Life door, since that is the one the Navs have historically emphasized most."

"What if I wasn't a part of a ministry that taught a particular door?"

"Then I'd probably still encourage you to begin with the Spirit-filled life."

"I suppose you're going to tell me why."

I smiled. "I suppose I am! I think the Spirit-filled door is one of the easiest to share with new believers. Especially the simple way Dr. Bright explains it in the Holy Spirit booklet. Some of the others, particularly the position door, are more doctrinally complex. In my experience new believers sometimes have trouble understanding it."

"I know what you mean," Emily agreed. "I've actually been frustrated that some of my women have struggled with it. One said it sounded like science fiction!"

"There you go," I said. "My practice is to begin with the Spirit-filled door and only move on to one of the others if it becomes clear that one of my disciples just isn't finding the first door helpful."

"Well, thanks, Alan. I can't wait . . ." Emily paused and got a funny look on her face.

"What?" I said.

She laughed. "I just caught myself. I was about to say, 'I can't wait to share this doors-into-faith concept with my girls.' But I suppose that would be a mistake, wouldn't it? I'd be sharing what I need instead of what they need."

Emily was struggling with a delicate balance that is a challenge to every Christian worker. We need to gently help new believers along. We need to help them take baby steps before we challenge them to jump or run. At different times in our lives, different doors may be more effective ways to enter into faith. Clearly for Emily, it was time to learn about the position door. Ideally we should grasp a number of doors for the sake of our own maturing and continued stable walk. Years from now Emily may well have the same experience with the position door. To keep her own walk vital, she may need to focus on the grace door or the brokenness door. But for her own disciples she probably needs to pick a door and help them master it until they are walking consistently.

Help Many Kinds of Believers Find Their Best Door

My wife, Jan, had a brilliant idea. It was certainly not the first time this had happened in our thirty years of marriage, and I'm sure it will not be the last! It was two summers ago, as we were discussing my desire to write this book.

"Why don't we pull together a small group of Christians from our community here in the mountains?" she suggested. "We could meet on a certain evening, read together the pages you've written that week, and discuss them."

One of the first people we challenged to join the group was Mike Beavers. Mike is a licensed marriage and family therapist whom we had known as a friend for many years. More recently Mike had become a colleague teaching counseling classes at the seminary where I teach.

Mike gave me a ride home after classes one day, and I explained the idea for the book. I concluded by sharing my hypothesis that basic personality, family background, and church experience can affect which of the doors is most likely to work for each individual. He became quite excited.

"You know, we could put together a controlled study—design a questionnaire. First, give them some standard personality tests and then see how those correlate to the door they've found helpful."

It was an intriguing idea. In the end we decided it was too complex and massive a project to pull off properly in the time I had to write this book. But I'd still like to do the study someday. Although the number of factors involved make the investment of time and money required to do it right rather daunting.

Instead, I have drawn on the experience of more than thirty years of ministry on four continents. In addition, we did pull together the group, just as Jan had suggested. We've met weekly for the past eighteen months as I've been writing the book. It turned out to be quite a diverse group. The age ranged from some in their twenties to those in their sixties. Some were married, others single or widowed. Some had been raised in Christian homes; others had come to Christ later in life. What we looked for (and found) were Christians who were articulate and serious about developing a deeper walk with God. Just as I'd hoped, as we went through each of the doors, someone in the group would always say, "This is a door that has really helped me." And often, we'd have the opposite reaction as well. "This is definitely not my door!" Then as a group we would explore and discuss the reasons why a particular door had or had not been helpful.

Workshopping the book with the group has gone a long way toward confirming my previous observations in ministry. I think there are a number of factors that influence which door is likely to be the most helpful door for you.

One thing that may powerfully influence which door fits you best is simply your God-given temperament and personality. Are you an optimist like me? Do you generally look forward to the future and naturally expect the best from others, yourself, and even God? Then you may be attracted to the more "positive" doors: grace, Spirit-filled, or positional truth. One thing these three doors have in common is they ask us to believe something positive. God loves me unconditionally (grace). He sees me as already perfect (position). I can have God's supernatural power (Spirit-filled).

But what if you're more like my wife, Jan, a pessimist? (Or, as she prefers, a "realist.") Are you good at anticipating things that might go wrong? Do you look to the future with caution? Are you slower to trust yourself, others, and even God? Then you may gravitate toward the more "negative" doors: discipline, brokenness, or the exchanged life. Each of these doors requires a certain mistrust of myself. I must admit that my natural instincts are ungodly and undisciplined. I must allow my self-confidence to be broken by life's trials. I must get out of the way so Christ's life can flow out from me.

But that is only one dimension of personality. God has made us multifaceted. Are you outgoing or quiet? Are you detail-oriented or an abstract generalist? Are you more motivated by achievement or relationships? Are you high-strung or placid? Do you tend toward black-white thinking or are you having trouble answering these questions? Any of these aspects of the way God has made you may affect which doors are most helpful.

The temperaments and parenting styles of your parents can also have a powerful impact on how you relate to God and therefore what kind of door will work best for you. Were your parents demanding or lenient? Were they warm and caring or distant and indifferent? Psychologists tell us we develop an unconscious picture of God from a blend of those who parented us (and to a lesser degree from our siblings and extended family members). You might try this experiment. Next time you are alone with God, try to figure out what your mental image is of the One to whom you are praying. Do you picture him sitting next to you in the room or is he sitting on a throne far above you? Is he smiling or does he have a stern look on his face? Are you even picturing a person at all? Or is God more like a cloud or a dense fog? Now, once you have the picture firmly in mind, try to figure out what qualities that you picture in God are similar to those in the ones who raised you.

The parental-style factor can be a little tricky when it comes to predicting which door will be the most helpful. It may seem logical that if a woman had parents who were highly organized or even perfectionistic, then she would gravitate toward the discipline or maybe the brokenness door. And sometimes it works that way. However it can be just the opposite. Two individuals in our small group had great difficulty relating to both the discipline and brokenness doors. Both had parents who were demanding and even physically abusive. It took the grace or Spirit-filled doors for them to even be able to begin to trust God and walk with him.

Beyond personality and upbringing there are other factors that may influence your choice in doors. If you were raised in or found Christ in a church or movement that emphasized a certain door, it is likely that door will tend to feel comfortable and natural to you. But again the opposite is sometimes true. If you had a bad experience in a particular church or Christian group, there may be an emotional barrier later in life toward anything the group taught, including any doors into faith.

Can you begin to see why I didn't immediately jump on Mike's idea of a questionnaire to determine what makes a door best for each individual? There are so many factors and they work in combination. That is why I am usually not able to determine in advance which door will work for an individual. As I suggested to Emily, I usually begin with one door (in my case, walking in the Spirit) and move on to others only if that one does not appear to be working.

However, as a Christian worker, I feel it is crucial for me to be familiar with as many of these doors as possible. I want to be able to help many different kinds of believers to begin and continue to grow in their faith walk. So I need to be able to present several very different kinds of doors, including those that do not attract me and may not be helpful to me personally.

And, as Emily discovered, a particular door may be more useful at one point in life than it is in others. When I went through the wrenching event I recounted in chapter 4, it was very helpful that I already understood, at least in theory, the brokenness door. I suspect the whole process could have taken a lot longer and been even more painful if I had not already had a basic understanding of how God might use pain and suffering to strengthen my faith.

Don't Give Up Hope

"I've decided I must be a spiritual reject."

Willy's face was nearly blank. His words were desperate, but he said them in almost a monotone.

"At one time or another I've tried all these 'doors' as you call them. Usually I start out feeling hopeful. I desperately pray that this is the one that will do it for me. But sooner or later it's always the same. God is just as far away as ever."

"That sounds pretty dreadful," I said.

"And do you know what's the worst part?"

I shook my head.

"Every time I try another 'secret to the Christian life' and it doesn't work, I get more discouraged. Frankly I'm at the point now that if something new came along, I'm not sure I'd even want to try it."

Maybe you're like Willy. Maybe you began this book with a sense of hope (as perhaps you've approached previous books, seminars, and sermons). But maybe you're pretty sure by now that none of the six doors I've covered is "your door." What should you do if you still haven't found a door that works for you?

Please, I beg you, don't give up hope as Willy did. To begin with, there are many more than six doors offered in the Bible. (In fact I'm pretty sure I haven't found all of them yet!) But let me suggest a few places you can look in the Scriptures.

In Hebrews 11, which some have called the "Hall of Faith," we find eighteen Old Testament characters mentioned by name and many more indicated less directly. Each of these is held up as a model of faith. In some cases the writer is probably talking about saving faith, but in many cases it is clear that these men and women walked by faith over a long period of time.

So my suggestion is this. Try spending some time reading the biblical accounts of these men and women of faith. See if some of their experiences can't serve as "doors into faith" for you.

Another way to find more doors is to do a systematic study of one of the books of the Bible where faith is a major theme. As I mentioned before, Hebrews, Galatians, Romans, and Joshua are four such books. You can do a study of one of these books by yourself, with a partner, or in a small group. What I'm suggesting is not terribly complex. Before you begin, pray for the Holy Spirit to help you understand what you are reading. As you read the particular book of the Bible, just mark every verse that either mentions the words *faith* or *believe* and also every verse that seems to be teaching something about faith, even if it doesn't use the word. After you've identified about ten to fifteen verses on faith, stop and try to put the verses together in categories. Which ones seem to be talking about related aspects of faith?

Eventually, as you continue this process, you will begin to develop your own theology of faith. And you may begin to discover one or more additional doors into faith.

Remember, a door into faith is any sound biblical teaching that assists you (or someone else) in actually beginning or continuing a walk of faith.

Reform Your Image of God

Before I leave this subject I want to explore some of the reasons why some Christians find it very difficult to walk by faith, even when they clearly understand one or more biblical doors. I've mentioned several times in this book that we develop an unconscious image of God from our early caregivers. But what if a child's parents (or stepparents) verbally, physically, or even sexually abuse him or her? Though the person may genuinely receive Christ as Savior, his or her unconscious picture of God may be so distorted that trust is extremely difficult if not impossible. I'm not saying the conscious intellectual view of God is distorted. The person may have had sound Christian teaching. He or she may know intellectually that God is patient, kind, loving, and trustworthy. But when the person prays, his or her heart says something different. The person is afraid to trust. His or her emotional, unconscious image of God may be too much like that giant man who used to come into the room late at night and leave him or her sobbing.

But how can anyone change an image that was formed in childhood? As a professor of theology, I wish I could tell you that the answer is to take theology classes at your local seminary! But, sadly, formal study of theology does little to change our emotional, unconscious God-image.

"What's the answer, Linda?" I asked. "How can someone learn to trust God and walk by faith if they have serious emotional trust issues that come from childhood?"

Linda Parker was one of my colleagues at the International School of Theology. Among her other accomplishments, Linda was (and is) a licensed Marriage, Family, and Child counselor (MFCC) in the state of California and has an extensive private practice. We were privileged to have her teach several counseling classes to our men and women preparing for ministry.

For several years Linda and I had invited each other to guest lecture in our classes. I'd tell her students about the counseling implications of theology and she'd talk to my students about the theological importance of counseling. This led to many discussions about where the two fields overlapped.

Linda thought for a moment. "I think the simplest way to answer your question is to say that people created the emotional problem and people are going to be a large part of the solution."

"Are you talking about years of professional counseling?"

"Not necessarily," Linda said. "In less severe cases, a close relationship with a caring Christian friend who models the love of God may be all it takes."

"Why does that help?" I asked. "I mean, I believe in the power of God's Word and the power of prayer, but why is the one-on-one setting helpful?"

"When two people, especially same-gender friends, spend a lot of time together, an intimacy and trust is often formed. It can be very powerful if a woman, let's say, who fears and mistrusts God, can spend time in prayer with a mature Christian friend who is walking closely with the Lord. The fearful woman can, over time, begin to see God through her friend's own experience of God's love. Pretty soon the friend's ability to receive and give God's love helps the fearful woman begin to trust."

"Okay," I said, "I understand we're talking about what we might call milder cases of mistrust."

"That's right."

"What about a somewhat more difficult situation?"

"Then I usually recommend a support group of some kind. Maybe made up of others who have a similar background or have struggled with similar problems."

"But don't you run the danger of reinforcing the wrong attitudes?"

"Yes," Linda admitted. "But maybe not as great a danger as you might think. However, it is best if there can be a trained and experienced leader or group facilitator. It's also important to have at least one or two in the group who are further along in working through their issues to set a positive and constructive tone."

"And what about the more difficult cases of mistrust? Then are we talking about professional help?"

"Probably. Often it takes more time and specialized training than most pastors are likely to have. And usually formal counseling is most effective when the client is also in a good support group."

"And how long are we talking? In the more difficult cases, I mean."

"Well, I guess the honest answer is as long as it takes. It might be a number of months, but in severe cases, where childhood sexual abuse is involved, for example, we might be talking about years."

"Ouch!" I said.

"But the point is," Linda continued, "that it's the body of Christ the Holy Spirit uses to reform a damaged God-image. It's still relationships in the body, whether we are talking a professional Christian counselor or simply a loving Christian friend."

* * *

My Hope for You

In this book we've explored together a number of biblical doors designed by our heavenly Father to open into the greatest adventure the human spirit can know in this earthly life—a daily, hourly, moment-by-moment walk of faith. I hope you have found a door that will open for you. And if you've already been using one of the doors, I hope you've expanded your understanding and appreciation of faith.

After thirty years using these doors, I feel that I'm only beginning to grab hold of all that God has for me in the panorama of faith into which these doors open. And, of course, thirty years *is* only a tiny beginning. I've suggested our earthly walk of faith is just a brief transition period, a little like engagement. But a full-orbed life of faith will be our path for all eternity. The longest earthly life of the greatest man of faith (Abraham, Moses, David?) would really only be a few short steps on an eternal journey that will eventually take us to realms beyond our imagination.

It's a perfect day for an adventure. Won't you join me?

APPENDIX

DEFECTIVE DOORS

Popular Errors about Faith

The six doors I have covered in this book are all what I would call genuine biblical doors into faith. If you understand what the Bible says about any one of these doors and approach it with the right attitude, you will be able to enter into a life of faith.

Unfortunately, there are also a number of popular teachings about faith and the Christian life that include theological or biblical errors. I think of these as "broken" or "defective" doors. I'm not talking about cultic teaching or non-Christian religions. Instead, I mean teachings promoted by sincere teachers, most (if not all) of whom are themselves born-again believers. These teachers preach a gospel of salvation by grace through faith alone. But when it comes to instructing Christians on how to live the Christian life, they run into serious problems.

The fact that these teachers include biblical errors in their teaching is bad enough, but that is not the only reason I call these teachings "defective doors." These teachings also create practical problems for those unsuspecting Christians who try to enter a life of faith by means of these broken doors.

I want to take a closer look at three of these defective doors and explain how they can make it harder to enter a consistent lifelong walk of faith.

Beyond Sin?—Wesleyan Perfectionism

"It is possible for mature believers to reach the point where they no longer intentionally sin. We call this 'utter sanctification' or 'Christian perfection' and it should be one of the goals we all strive for in this earthly life."

My oldest daughter, Becky, sat in her religion class and couldn't believe her ears. She was attending a Christian college and the college chaplain, a Nazarene minister, was teaching this required class.

After class, Becky went up to talk to the professor.

"Were you really saying that we can become sinlessly perfect in this life?"

"Perfect, yes," the chaplain replied. "The 'sinless' part would depend on how you define sin."

"I've never heard this teaching before. Where does it come from?"

The professor smiled. "I believe it comes from the Bible. But the person in church history who popularized it was John Wesley."

"Really!" Becky thought a moment. "Could I do my term paper on John Wesley's view of Christian perfection?"

"Sure. I think that would be an excellent topic for a paper."

As Becky researched the paper, she learned that her professor was right. John Wesley did teach that a kind of Christian perfection was possible in this earthly life. She also discovered that Wesley's view is still widely believed and taught by many traditional Methodist, Wesleyan, and Nazarene ministers and writers.

What exactly do Wesley and his followers mean by Christian perfection? Let me begin by saying what they don't believe. They do not believe that Christians can reach the point in this life where they are absolutely holy in thought, word, and deed. They also do not believe that an individual can ever reach absolute spiritual maturity where there is no longer any room for growth.

What Wesleyans do believe is that it is possible to reach a point in the Christian life where we will no longer intentionally choose to sin. We may still commit unintentional sins of omission (honestly overlooking something we later realize we should have done). We may also still make naive mistakes. We will never reach the point in this life where we have a guarantee we will always do exactly what Christ would do in every situation. But we can reach the point where we will never choose to do wrong, if we know it is wrong. That is what Wesleyans mean by total sanctification or Christian perfection.

You may remember that in chapter 8 I talked about the biblical concept of "unknown unrighteousness." First John 1:7, 9 teaches that Jesus' blood cleanses us from those "sins" or areas of unrighteousness that we are not even aware of. But these passages also teach that we must consciously confess any intentional sins. When we willfully think, say, or do something we know is wrong, the Holy Spirit is grieved and our fellowship with God is temporarily hindered. What Wesleyans believe is that some Christians eventually become mature enough that they are incapable of choosing to do something they know is wrong.

Well, what about it? Is it possible to get to the point in this life where we make only unintentional errors but will never again consciously disobey God? Without going into Wesley's argument in detail, let me say in a general way where I think he was mistaken. A lot of Wesley's argument for this teaching rests on the following line of reasoning: God would not be so unfair as to command us to do something that was impossible. There are many places in the Bible where God commands us to live righteous and holy lives. Therefore it must be possible.

I have two basic problems with this Wesleyan argument. The first is that it proves too much. Let's just take one of the verses Wesleyans frequently quote. During the Sermon on the Mount, Jesus said, "You are to be perfect, as your heavenly Father is perfect" (Matt. 5:48). So, Wesleyans argue, if Jesus commanded perfection, it must be possible. But take a closer look at the kind of perfection Jesus commands in this verse. We are to be as perfect as God! As we've already seen, Wesley did not think any Christian would ever become absolutely holy in every respect in this life. But God's holiness is absolute, isn't it? And if we are to be holy as he is holy, wouldn't that mean absolute holiness? What this says to me is there is something wrong with the argument that if God commands something, then it must be possible in this life. Wesley's argument proves more than he wants to prove!

My second problem with the Wesleyan view is I believe there are Scriptures that teach we will always be capable of choosing to sin until we die. Just before John's frequently quoted verse on confession, we find an important statement. "If we say we have no sin, we are deceiving ourselves, and the truth is not in us" (1 John 1:8).

I believe every biblical error carries with it one or more practical consequences. God did not put theology in the Bible primarily to satisfy our curiosity but rather to help us know him better and walk with him more closely.

Therefore, I want to talk for a minute about the practical difficulties with the Wesleyan view. I've called this view a defective door because I think it presents some unnecessary barriers to a consistent walk of faith.

My first problem with this view is that it sets up two classes of believers: the haves and the have-nots. I think this can be a barrier to faith for both groups. For new believers (and even more for older believers who know quite well they are still capable of conscious sin), it gives them a sense that they are second-class Christians. God can't really use them yet because they haven't had the second blessing or "second work of grace."[1] While Wesley intended this teaching to spur Christians on toward holiness, I've seen it work the other way. I've talked to Wesleyan and Nazarene Christians who said, "Since I'm not really going to have victory over sin until I reach utter sanctification, what's the point of fighting it now? I'm going to lose anyway. I might just as well give in and not put myself through the struggle."

This teaching can also create problems for older believers who think they have reached perfection. It puts incredible pressure on them to never fail in anything. And those who know they are still capable of sin can easily feel self-conscious or even question the Lord. "Why have I been a Christian so long and still don't have this second blessing?" Some may even be afraid to admit to other believers that they don't yet have it.

I think all of these attitudes hinder a real walk of faith. The essence of faith is to take the focus entirely off myself and my maturity or lack of it. Faith is putting my eyes on Christ, accepting that even in my unacceptable state, he has accepted me, and basking in the joy of his undeserved favor.

My own view is that this idea of Christian perfection is a kind of chimera or phantom, and a dangerous one. Paul warned, "Let him who thinks he stands take heed lest he fall" (1 Cor. 10:12). To me the best way to keep on walking in faith is to realize every day I am still a sinner saved by God's grace.

Although I think all the defective doors carry unnecessary hindrances to a real walk of faith, some are more severely broken than others. I have covered the least dangerous of the three defective doors first. I am certain that many Wesleyan Christians do find a consistent walk of faith despite the unbiblical aspects of their teaching on sanctification. Many poorly made and badly hung doors can still be opened with some effort. By God's grace many still make it through the defective Wesleyan door into the true attitude of faith.

Spirit Baptized?—Classic Pentecostalism

"I guess I'm not a very good Pentecostal." Samantha looked at me sideways with a hint of a wry smile lifting one corner of her mouth. We had been dating for about a month. I was a new believer, but she had been raised in a traditional Pentecostal church.

"Why do you say that?" I asked.

"Well, I was saved when I was seven and got the baptism and spoke in tongues when I was twelve."

"What's wrong with that?"

"Nothing, but my church teaches that any believers who don't yet have the baptism can't really have God's power. And it's the job of us who do to encourage them to seek it."

"I guess that makes sense," I said.

"But I don't do that." She gave me another wry smile. "Haven't you noticed I haven't bugged you to seek the baptism, even though you've never spoken in tongues?"

"I hadn't thought about it," I said. "But you're right. You've never brought it up. How come?"

"I believed all that stuff about the baptism and God's power until I got to high school."

"What happened?"

"I got involved with Youth for Christ. I went to several of their conferences and retreats. I heard some wonderful speakers. And none of them emphasized tongues or the baptism. I'm sure most of them had never spoken in tongues. But I could see the fruit of the Spirit in their lives and some of them had led hundreds, even thousands, of kids to the Lord. It was pretty hard to deny they had God's power, maybe more than I did."

Samantha sighed. "So I guess I'm a lousy Pentecostal."

In my estimation the classic Pentecostal view Samantha was taught is another broken door into faith. And I consider it a somewhat more serious error than the Wesleyan view. It's interesting that historically the Pentecostal position grew out of and was influenced by Wesleyan teaching. Pentecostalism began early in the twentieth century and was influenced by the holiness movement of the nineteenth century, which in turn developed out of early Methodism.

Following Wesley, Pentecostals teach that there is a second work of grace or a second blessing subsequent to salvation. However, Pentecostals see this second event in the Christian life normally happening early in Christian experience rather than late. Pentecostals call this second blessing the "baptism of the Holy Spirit." They believe the baptism confers spiritual power, including greater power to resist sin. But most Pentecostals do not believe that a Spirit-baptized believer is free from volitional sin. In classic Pentecostal teaching, the experience of speaking in tongues always accompanies the baptism of the Holy Spirit. Therefore, a true Pentecostal can ask another Christian, "Have you ever spoken in tongues?" If the person answers no, the Pentecostal knows that he or she has not had the bap-

tism and doesn't have the full power God intends for every
Christian.

What's wrong with this view? First, I do not believe it
is biblical. I believe 1 Corinthians 12:13 teaches all true
believers receive the baptism of the Spirit at the moment
they become Christians.[2]

This defective door shares some of the problems of the
Wesleyan teaching. It creates two classes of Christians,
those who have the baptism and those who don't. But the
reason this broken door concerns me more than the Wesleyan teaching is because Pentecostals see the second blessing happening earlier in a Christian's experience. New
Wesleyan Christians normally would not be concerned
that they'd not yet received utter sanctification since that
is usually reserved for mature believers. But a new believer
in a Pentecostal church will often experience great pressure to "seek the baptism."

I see this emphasis as a potential hindrance to faith for
both those who have had the baptism and those who
haven't. Those who have not spoken in tongues are told
they can't really have God's power until they do. If new
believers accept this idea, there is little motivation to try
to walk by faith until they receive the blessing.

But what about those who do have some kind of emotional experience and speak in tongues? No doubt many
of them are given a short-term boost in their ability to trust
God and walk by faith. But for many it is at the expense
of ever developing a long-term consistent walk. I've
known quite a number of Pentecostals for whom the emotional experience is so overwhelming that they find it hard
to believe they are close to God unless they've had a similar experience in the last day or two. The experience
becomes a necessary ingredient for faith. If it's been a week
or two since the last experience, it seems impossible for
them to trust God.

I want to clarify something that may be potentially confusing. My criticisms of this broken door apply primarily to those who teach the strict Pentecostal position.[3] Many charismatic churches have been influenced by Pentecostal teaching but are not as dogmatic that the baptism of the Holy Spirit is separate from salvation or must always be accompanied by an emotional experience or by speaking in tongues. Charismatic movements such as Calvary Chapel and the Vineyard have put a greater emphasis on prayer, worship, and Bible study and less on the baptism as the sole key to spiritual power. For example, listen to the recent words of Chuck Smith, founder of Calvary Chapel. After acknowledging that the baptism of the Holy Spirit can be concurrent with salvation, he goes on to say he's not hung up on terminology. "Some call it baptism. Some call it being filled with the Spirit. It doesn't matter what you call it, the main thing is that you have it."[4]

As is true for many Wesleyans, many Pentecostals manage to walk through their defective door and find a real life of faith. Many more, in my experience, never manage to get through the door or find it a difficult door to use long term.

Healthy and Wealthy (Name It and Claim It) Teachers

Even more dangerous than the previous doors is the teaching that God intends all believers to be healthy and rich. Oddly enough this broken door is also historically connected to the other two. A very vocal minority of Pentecostal preachers and evangelists over the past forty years have embraced what some have called the "name it and claim it" approach to living the Christian life. Among the best-known promoters of this defective door are Kenneth Hagin, Kenneth Copeland, and Benny Hinn.

These teachers proclaim that God wants every Christian to be both healthy and rich. If you know Christ and you are poor or sick, it's evidence of your own lack of faith. They argue this view primarily from God's promises to Israel in the Old Testament and selected sayings of Jesus in the Gospels.

Their arguments are so theologically naive I hardly know where to begin. The problem with most of the Old Testament verses they cite is that these were promises to the nation of Israel under a theocratic government. Christians today cannot simplistically claim these promises any more than a contemporary childless couple can claim for themselves God's promise to Abraham that he would make of Abraham's seed a great nation. As for the words of Jesus, the faith teachers are highly selective in which statements they quote, to say the least! In chapter 4 we looked at the many times Jesus and his disciples promised the Christian life on this earth would be filled with hardship, persecution, pain, and death.

I'm convinced that a dangerous teaching like the health and wealth gospel could have originated only in a relatively stable country with a Christian heritage like the United States. In America it seems to make sense to say that if you follow biblical ethics and trust God, you will become wealthy. Ours is a stable economy where hard work and honesty will often lead to an improvement in your economic status. But what about Christians in Iraq today? What about believers in the Soviet Union for most of the twentieth century? What about faithful Christians in the majority of non-Western societies for most of the last two thousand years? In most cases, if they really trusted God, they would experience economic persecution and (for the leaders at least) prison and an early death!

These teachers also claim that the Bible promises healing for everyone who has faith. There are many passages that make it clear that sometimes God heals and other times he does not, regardless of the faith of the humans involved. But let me give just one example.

There is little doubt that Paul, the apostle to the Gentiles, was a man of extraordinary faith. And yet he tells us he had an agonizing physical problem he calls his "thorn in the flesh" (2 Cor. 12:7). He tells us he pleaded with God three times to take it away. How does this story end? With Paul miraculously healed? After all, he healed others and even raised one man from the dead! No, the story ends rather differently. Paul receives a message directly from God. And what does God say? We know exactly what God told Paul because Paul quotes him for us. God said, "My grace is sufficient for you, for power is perfected in weakness" (v. 9). Listen to what Paul learned from this incident. "Therefore I am well content with weaknesses, with insults, with distresses, with persecutions, with difficulties, for Christ's sake; for when I am weak, then I am strong" (v. 10).

Of the three we've examined, this defective door is the most dangerous to a life of consistent faith. Imagine what happens to people who trust God to heal them or trust God to make them rich and then the opposite happens. According to these teachers, the problem is simply that they do not have enough faith. So now, in addition to being sicker or poorer, these hurting believers are carrying the emotional burden of guilt that their lack of faith is responsible for their sad condition. How likely are other believers to help them or comfort them as the Bible says we should do? After all, it's their own fault they're in such a mess!

"But what about those who do get better or do get a pay raise?" you may be asking. "Won't it encourage their faith?" Perhaps, for a time. The problem is that this sort of faith is a kind of time bomb. Even if things go well for weeks, months, or years, sooner or later the sin loose in this fallen world is going to catch up with them and they're going to have troubles no amount of prayer or faith can fix. Then what happens to their walk with God?

John Detrick, my best man when Jan and I were married, has been blind since birth. John and I met in college and sang and played guitar together for a number of years. John has an incredibly moving testimony about how God took this nerdy blind kid who felt sorry for himself and transformed his life. Since college John has served the Lord in full-time ministry and is now the senior pastor of a church in northern California. For forty years God has used the combination of John's blindness and contagious faith to bring many into the kingdom.

Before I met John, when he was still in high school, he was invited to perform at a music and healing service of the prominent Pentacostal singer and songwriter, Audrey Mieir. When the crowds had gone, the evangelist came over to John. After thanking him for his music, she asked him a question. "John, do you believe God can heal you?"

"Yes, ma'am, I know my God can heal me."

"John, do you believe God *will* heal you?"

"No, Miss Mieir, I do not believe he will heal me."

"I'm surprised. You seem so certain."

"I am. You see, I believe God will get greater glory shining through my blindness than he would by healing me physically."

John paused. "Besides, Miss Mieir, I'm going to have a great privilege even you won't have."

"What is that?"

"The first face I will ever see is the face of my glorious Savior."

NOTES

Chapter 1: Just a Closer Walk with Thee

1. Brittany is not her real name. Although all the conversations in this book are real, I have changed the names and disguised incidental details to protect the privacy of the individuals. Generally, if I give only the first name of a person (like Brittany), it is a pseudonym. In some cases I had several conversations with an individual on the same topic and for ease of reading have combined the essence of these into one conversation. In a few cases I had a number of similar exchanges with different people on the same subject and have chosen to portray these as one conversation with one person. When the full name is used (such as for my friend Blair Cook in chapter 6) the name is real and the incident is recounted with the permission of the person named. I have also used the real names of my wife, my children, and their spouses.

2. I would likely try to refer her to a competent medical doctor and, perhaps, a Christian psychiatrist.

3. Good books for nonbelievers include Josh McDowell, *More than a Carpenter* (Wheaton: Tyndale, 1977); and Gregory and Edward Boyd, *Letters from a Skeptic* (Colorado Springs: Chariot Victor, 1994). You may even be able to find a copy of my first book *The Artful Dodger: A Skeptic Confronts Christianity* (San Bernardino: Here's Life, 1981). The book is out of print but often available through used book sites such as Amazon.com.

4. The engagement took place in October 1999 and they were married the following July.

Chapter 2: How Much Faith Is Enough?

1. The NIV is nearly identical: "For the love of money is a root of all kinds of evil."

Chapter 3: Door 1

1. Some have interpreted Paul to be saying that at the moment of conversion, God supernaturally adds some new constitutional element to the human

makeup. Others think Paul is referring to a new orientation or relationship that is established in the new birth.

2. I have developed my own view of the new self, or new nature, in *The Artful Dodger*, 125–36.

3. The choice in the mall that day was not a difficult one. I was in the initial euphoria of engagement. I wish I could say that every day since then I have made the same choice, easily and consistently, but I have not. Likewise, it sometimes seems harder for one who has been a Christian a long time to keep his or her focus on the Lord than it is for those still in the first excitement of becoming a Christian.

4. Watchman Nee, *Sit, Walk, Stand* (Wheaton, Ill.: Tyndale House, 1977), 19.

5. Neil T. Anderson, *The Bondage Breaker* (Eugene, Ore.: Harvest House, 1990), 190.

6. Ibid., 217.

7. Ibid., 191, 208–9.

Chapter 4: Door 2

1. My two older brothers, John and David, were killed in a car accident before I was two years old. I now believe that this tragedy was a contributing factor to my father's emotional distance from me.

2. Spock's classic, *Baby and Child Care,* became the biggest-selling book after the Bible in U.S. history, with nearly fifty million copies sold since its first appearance in 1946.

3. It is clear from his words in Gethsemane that Jesus (who is God) did not always get everything he wanted. "If you are willing, take this cup from me; yet not my will, but yours be done" (Luke 22:42 NIV.) I think it would also have been the perfect will of God the Father to give his beloved Son what he asked. In this case, both the Father and the Son had to settle for their permissive will to achieve the salvation of the human race.

4. L. E. Maxwell, *Born Crucified: The Cross in the Life of the Believer* (Chicago: Moody, 1945).

5. Roy Hession, *The Calvary Road* (Fort Washington, Pa.: Christian Literature Crusade, 1971).

6. Norman Grubb, "Continuous Revival" (Fort Washington, Pa: Christian Literature Crusade, 1971).

7. Watchman Nee, *The Release of the Spirit* (Sure Foundation, 1965).

8. Dan Haseltine, "Worlds Apart," *Jars of Clay* (Brentwood, Tenn.: Brentwood Music Publishing, 1995).

9. Dan Haseltine, Steve Mason, Matt Odmark, and Charlie Lowell, "Frail," *Much Afraid* (Nashville: Brentwood-Benson Music Publishing, 1994).

Chapter 5: Door 3

1. Udo is a son-in-law of Francis Schaeffer and was teaching a series on Christian Worldview at this, the first series of International School Project convocations held in May 1991.

2. "Peace I leave with you; My peace I give to you; not as the world gives, do I give to you. Let not your heart be troubled, nor let it be fearful."

3. A similar idea is communicated by the word translated "guardians" *(epitropos)* in Galatians 4:2 NIV.

4. Generally women did not receive academic education at all and younger sons might receive only a basic education or be given training in a trade. Education in math, language, philosophy, history, etc. was most often reserved for the firstborn son who would inherit the bulk of the father's wealth and responsibility.

5. Moral Re-Armament (also known as the Oxford Group) was founded by Frank Buckman (1878–1961). While generally Christian, the movement was nondenominational and stressed world and societal change through individual morality.

6. Steve McVey, *Grace Rules* (Eugene, Ore.: Harvest House, 1998), 10.

7. Ibid., 13.

8. Charles R. Swindoll, *The Grace Awakening* (Dallas: Word, 1990), 76.

9. Philip Yancey, *What's So Amazing about Grace?* (Grand Rapids: Zondervan, 1997), 207.

10. Ibid., 210.

Chapter 6: Door 4

1. Some might say it was just coincidence. Maybe I would have remembered my jacket even if I hadn't turned the search over to Christ. I must confess that skeptical idea did pass through my head shortly after I found the keys. Perhaps that's why I so often have to exhaust my own resources before I'm willing to empty myself and let Christ take over.

2. A number of Christian authors have called this understanding of sanctification the exchanged life. See Major W. Ian Thomas, *The Saving Life of Christ* (Grand Rapids: Zondervan, 1961), 25, 43; and John Hunter, *Knowing God's Secrets* (Grand Rapids: Zondervan, 1965), 26.

3. Later, in 1991, that airline went broke and disbanded.

4. A. B. Simpson, *The Self Life and the Christ Life* (Harrisburg, Pa.: Christian Publications, 1950), 9.

5. Ibid., 11.

6. Major W. Ian Thomas, *The Saving Life of Christ* (Grand Rapids: Zondervan, 1961), 15.

7. Ibid., 150–51. Other influential presentations of this view of the Christian life by Thomas include *The Mystery of Godliness* and *If I Perish, I Perish.*

8. John Hunter, *Knowing God's Secrets* (Grand Rapids: Zondervan, 1965), and *Living the Christ-Filled Life* (Grand Rapids: Zondervan, 1969), D. Stuart Briscoe, *The Fullness of Christ* (Grand Rapids: Zondervan, 1965).

9. I've ended up in both Norilsk and Murmansk, Russia, as a result of phone calls from Blair.

Chapter 7: Door 5

1. Some might argue that money is intrinsically evil. However, as I pointed out in chapter 2, the Bible does not teach that money itself is bad, but rather the *love* of money is a root of evil (1 Tim. 3:3; 6:10; 2 Tim. 3:2; Heb. 13:5).

2. It was the tense incident where twenty-four Navy airplane crew members were downed in China in April 2001.

3. Lewis explored this idea rather fully in *The Great Divorce* (New York: Macmillan, 1946).

4. Richard J. Foster, *Celebration of Discipline*, rev. ed. (San Francisco: Harper, 1988), 6–7.

5. Dallas Willard, *The Spirit of the Disciplines* (San Francisco: Harper & Row, 1988), x.

6. Ibid., xii.

Chapter 8: Door 6

1. Bill Bright, "Have You Made the Wonderful Discovery of the Spirit-Filled Life?" (Orlando, Fla.: New Life Publications, 1966, 1995), 12.

2. The section on spiritual breathing was adapted from Bright, "Have You Made the Wonderful Discovery of the Spirit-Filled Life?" 15.

3. I personally do not agree with the Wesleyan teaching that it is possible to reach "entire sanctification" or Christian perfection in this life. Wesley did not teach that we could ever become "sinlessly perfect" but only that some believers reach a stage where they never again intentionally sin. (In the terms of this chapter, that would be continuous filling of the Spirit until death.) However, I believe the Scripture teaches that all believers are still capable of intentional sin every moment until they die and are finally released from their sin nature. I think that is what John is talking about in 1 John 1:8. See my further discussion of Wesleyan teaching in the appendix.

Chapter 9: Enter a Consistent Life of Faith

1. John Locke, *An Essay Concerning Human Understanding* (1690) and *The Reasonableness of Christianity* (1695).

2. For Locke the truth of the statements in the Bible is proven by the miracles of Moses and Jesus.

3. Trying to trace the exact nature and degree of Locke's influence on these thinkers, much less on contemporary Christian ideas of faith, would be a complex scholarly exercise far beyond the scope of this little book. The primary point I'm trying to make is that Locke-like views of faith are still with us.

4. In the nineteenth century these would include Princeton seminary professors Charles Hodge and B. B. Warfield. Twentieth-century rationalists include Norman Geisler, John Warwick Montgomery, Josh McDowell, and Gordon Lewis.

5. Søren [Johannes Climacus] Kierkegaard, *Philosophical Fragments or A Fragment of Philosophy*, trans. David F. Swenson; rev. trans. by Howard V. Hong (Princeton: Princeton University Press, 1962), 49, 118–19.

6. As in the case of Locke, I will not attempt to prove the extent of Kierkegaard's influence. He is widely acknowledged as the "father of existentialism" and influenced secular existentialists, such as Albert Camus and Jean-Paul Satre, as well as neo-orthodox and existential theologians, including Karl Barth, Emil Brunner, Rudolf Bultmann, and Paul Tillich.

7. Some evangelicals were directly or indirectly influenced by Kierkegaard. Others arrived at a similar a-rational view of faith for other reasons. Those who have a Kierkegaard-like view of faith include many Pentecostals, charismatics, and those Calvinists influenced by presuppositionalist Cornelius Van Til.

8. E. J. Carnell, *An Introduction to Christian Apologetics* (Grand Rapids: Eerdmans, 1948), 365. Carnell (1919–1967) was one of the founding faculty of Fuller Seminary and served as its second president.

9. The initial filling of the Spirit is a crisis, onetime event. But the concept of spiritual breathing is intended to produce an ongoing way of life.

10. I don't know who originated this statement. Some have suggested that Robert Munger coined it, but I have not found it in any of his published works.

11. Some might argue that grace holds a very central place in biblical teaching. That is true. However, most of the passages dealing with grace center on what God and Christ have done in being gracious to us. Grace is not given so central a prominence in discussions of our part in approaching God. We come to God by grace (his part) through faith (our part).

12. It is not so easy to demonstrate how discipline or brokenness are necessary ingredients of grace, for example.

Chapter 10: Almost Faith

1. The phrase "almost faith" was coined by my friend and colleague Ken Green.

2. For more on this idea see "Humanity: Good News and Bad News" in Alan Kent Scholes, *What Christianity Is All About: How You Can Know and Enjoy God* (Colorado Springs: NavPress, 1999), 95–106.

Chapter 11: Six Suggestions about Faith

1. Les Hughes, *The Sound of God's Applause* (Nashville: Broadman and Holman, 1999).

2. Steve McVey, *Grace Walk* (Eugene, Ore.: Harvest House, 1995); and *Grace Rules.*

Appendix: Defective Doors

1. *Second blessing* and *second work of grace* are both terms used in the Wesleyan tradition to refer to an experience subsequent to salvation that frees the believer from the ability to consciously sin. *Utter sanctification* and *Christian perfection* are also used to refer to this event, which most Wesleyans see as happening later in the Christian life after years of maturing.

2. For a somewhat more complete argument see Scholes, *What Christianity Is All About,* 209–10.

3. Three Pentecostal denominations that have traditionally taught this view are The Assemblies of God, The Foursquare Gospel, and The Open Bible churches.

4. Chuck Smith, *Calvary Chapel Distinctives* (Costa Mesa, Calif.: The Word for Today Publishers, 2000), 34–35.

Alan Scholes has been on the staff of Campus Crusade for Christ for more than thirty years. After having earned his Ph.D. from Claremont School of Theology, he has taught theology on four continents and served on the faculty of the International School of Theology and Talbot Seminary. He is the author of numerous articles and two previous books. He and his wife, Jan, have three grown children.